Four Modern Prophets

Walter Rauschenbusch
Martin Luther King, Jr.
Gustavo Gutiérrez
Rosemary Radford Ruether

William M. Ramsay

John Knox Press
LOUISVILLE

Library of Congress Cataloging-in-Publication Data

Ramsay, William M.
  Four modern prophets.

  Bibliography: p.
  1. Rauschenbusch, Walter, 1861–1918. 2. King, Martin Luther. 3. Gutierrez, Gustavo, 1928–   . 4. Ruether, Rosemary Radford. 5. Christian biography. 6. Church and social problems—History—20th century. I. Title.
BR1700.2.R35 1986   280'.092'2   [B]   86-45351
ISBN 0-8042-0811-5

© copyright John Knox Press 1986
10   9   8   7   6   5   4   3   2
Printed in the United States of America
John Knox Press
Louisville, Kentucky 40202-1396

To Orbis Press for excerpts from Gustavo Gutiérrez, *A Theology of Liberation: History, Politics and Salvation,* copyright 1973 Orbis Press, used by permission.

To Carl Rauschenbusch for excerpts from Walter Rauschenbusch, *Christianity and the Social Crisis* and *Christianizing the Social Order.*

Special thanks must go to the following for helpful comments and corrections which they have made on various parts of this manuscript:

Dr. Thomas R. Peake, Chair of the Social Science Division, King College, Bristol, TN, and a historian of the Southern Christian Leadership Conference, who commented on the chapter on Martin Luther King, Jr.

Dr. Robert McAfee Brown, Pacific School of Religion, Berkeley, CA, biographer of Gutiérrez and author of other books on liberation theology, who commented on the chapter on Gutiérrez.

Dr. Rosemary Radford Ruether, Garrett-Evangelical Theological Seminary, Evanston, IL, who commented on the chapter which deals with her own life and thought.

I am grateful, too, to Dr. Thomas D. Campbell and the other members of the committee which invited me to give the 1985 lectures at the Cumberland Presbyterian Ministers' Conference at Bethel College, McKenzie, TN. This book is based on those lectures.

Finally, thanks go to three Bethel College students who helped in the preparation of the manuscript: Mary Lou Ozee James, Stephanie Scrudder, and Allison Fountain.

Contents

In memory of my brother,
the Reverend Professor Charles McKay Ramsay, Ph.D., late
of Austin College, Sherman, Texas

One of his favorite texts was Numbers 11:29:
"Would that all the LORD's people were prophets, that the LORD
would put his spirit upon them!"

Introduction

Prophecy and the Twentieth Century—The full-color advertising brochure promised exciting applications of the word of God to our time. Being interested in the prophets myself, I quickly scanned the leaflet. The publisher should have known better. What they were advertising was one more book of fantastic speculations about "the rapture," "Armageddon," "the millennium," and how we are preparing for a last great battle. Soviet Russia, it seemed, would serve as the satanic army of darkness and we would be the army of light. The book promised to show how current events fit precisely into God's schedule and how all of these things are almost upon us now. Remembering the words of the risen Christ in Acts 1:7 that we are not supposed to know about the divine timetable I deposited the advertisement in the trash.

The idea of prophecy and the twentieth century, however, cannot be dismissed so lightly. What do the biblical prophets, Amos, Isaiah, Jeremiah, and the rest, really say to our time?

The New Testament tells us that there continued to be prophets in the early church. The prophets Agabus, Simon called Niger, Manaen, and others whose names we will never know spoke for

1

God to the first Christians. The author of Revelation was a prophet, and some biblical scholars suggest that many passages in our Gospels reflect anonymous prophetic utterances. What happened to this company of prophets is something of a mystery. Paul was certainly familiar with prophecy as one of the gifts of the Spirit. Did the Spirit later cease to inspire?

One suspects that, as the church grew and as more and more people began to preach and teach, too many erroneous predictions were made and too many heresies were uttered. Gnostics professing to be inspired prophets, Montanists claiming a direct line to the Holy Spirit, and others began to announce prophecies which too often turned out to be false. Eventually the church found it necessary to lay down some rules. An ecclesiastical hierarchy and a canon (rule) of Scripture were established. Prophets might continue to prophesy, but the value of their prophecies could, at least in part, be determined by checking their words against these standards. The canon provided guidelines and limits.

It is not wrong, therefore, to suggest that the Spirit may be inspiring prophets in the twentieth century. Indeed the preacher on Sunday morning modestly hopes not to be proclaiming his or her own wisdom but the very "word of God." Since the Spirit is not going to contradict what the Spirit has already inspired in the Scripture, we have at least one helpful way of judging just how authentically inspired a preacher or writer may be. The message of the canonical prophets should help us, at least with some limited degree of certainty, to spot a modern prophet should we meet one. We do not have much clear information about prophets in the New Testament church, but we know quite well the work of the Old Testament prophets. They give us models of prophecy. When someone today speaks forth for God in the Spirit which animated the work of Amos, Isaiah, and Jeremiah, we do well to listen. Their message of justice, wisely applied in that same Spirit, may indeed be thought of as God's prophetic word for our time. Jesus was more than a prophet, but he was a prophet. Most especially, therefore, when we find great teachers today calling upon us to share Christ's vision of the future, the coming kingdom of God, we may consider the possibility that we are hearing something very like prophets for our day.

This book is about four twentieth-century Christians who, in the broad sense of the term as we have described it, merit the honorable title "prophet." These authors would never claim that their works deserve a place in the canon. On the contrary, each claims merely to base his or her message in part on the words of Jesus and the canonical prophets. It is proposed here that the same Holy Spirit which inspired the biblical writers has enabled these four individuals to understand and present to us the ancient prophets' message of social justice for the twentieth century. It is, in that sense, therefore, genuine prophecy which we will examine.

If a prophet is simply one who speaks forth for God, then there are many, many prophets. Most of them, like most of those in the early church, bear names we will never know. The four "prophets" whose work is reviewed in this little volume have been selected because they have so effectively held up for us four different areas of concern. They have proclaimed God's demand for justice for four different groups of people.

(1) *Walter Rauschenbusch,* a child of German immigrants, ministered among poor working people in New York City. Early in the twentieth century he pioneered in a call for justice which became known as "the Social Gospel." Within this century, at least, almost every subsequent Christian call for social justice has been influenced by his work. Though from an earlier time than the others, he is included here because he so clearly articulated concerns which the others developed later.

(2) *Martin Luther King, Jr.* heard the prophetic call as he ministered in the Black ghetto of a southern city. In God's name he led the nation in making changes which, while still incomplete, have proved to be for Blacks and perhaps equally for their white oppressors a long "Stride Toward Freedom."

(3) *Gustavo Gutiérrez* lives thousands of miles further south, in Peru. His enunciation of "A Theology of Liberation" has been heard around the world. In it he has tried to express what the Spirit is now saying to and through the Latin American poor in their struggle for deliverance from oppression.

(4) *Rosemary Radford Ruether* is not Black, poor, or a third-world peasant. She is a middle-class North American white woman.

She reminds us, however, that the oppression of women is the oldest injustice in history. She has sought to present the light which the prophetic cry for justice sheds on the current movement for "Women's Liberation."

They are a varied group! Three are men; one is a woman. One is Hispanic, one is Black, and two have racial roots which go back to northern Europe. Two are Protestant (Baptist) and two are Roman Catholic. Ruether calls herself a liberal; Gutiérrez is so free of heresy that an investigation by the papal hierarchy could find no fault with his adherence to traditional doctrines.

One thing which unites these four is that they love the great biblical prophets and the call for right relationships among people which we find in Jesus. They are united in their call for social justice in God's name, even though each was called to apply that concern for justice to a different area, and they are united in that each has a vision of the future. Whatever else the prophets did, they made predictions. Each of the prophets we will examine spoke out of a hope, a dream, a vision of the coming of the kingdom of God.

This book is based on lectures which I delivered at the 1985 Ministers' Conference of the Cumberland Presbyterian Church at Bethel College in McKenzie, Tennessee. I had planned at first to speak abstractly on the subject of justice. It had been my privilege to help edit a paper entitled "Christian Faith and Economic Justice" which had been approved for study by the 1984 General Assembly of my own denomination, the Presbyterian Church (U.S.A.), and I had initially thought to develop systematically some of the ideas about justice presented in that document. Finally, however, I decided that I really could not add much that was not said better in that paper and that my efforts to do so would be pretty dull.

Instead it occurred to me that theologians today speak often of "the theology of story." The Bible is a book of stories. Before prophets such as Amos and Jeremiah had their words recorded in books God's people were telling stories. They told of Moses defying Pharaoh and crying in the name of the Lord, "Let my people go!" They told of the prophet Nathan seeing an injustice and pointing at King David to announce, "Thou art the man!" They told of the prophet Elijah who denounced King Ahab to his face when that tyrant had stolen a vineyard and condoned an illegal execution. They told the story of the prophet Elisha instigating a bloody political revolt against Queen Jezebel and her evil grandson on the throne.

What follows here, therefore, is four stories. Since God's word is always mediated through specific, individual women and men, we shall look, at least a little, not just at principles but at personalities. It is hoped that some part of the personality of each of these "prophets" will come through and give life to their messages.

Finally, a word of caution: none of these "prophets" would claim to be infallible. Even the predictions of the biblical prophets did not always come true in the ways they expected. The Northern Kingdom never was restored, nor was Ezekiel's ideal temple ever built. God had a better fulfillment planned than even those inspired prophets could have dreamed of. "For all the promises of God find their Yes in him" (2 Cor. 1:20). This book, therefore, does not at all intend to suggest that everything written by each of these four "prophets" is entirely true. That could not be the case for one obvious reason: they do not all agree. I have ventured to raise a question or two at the end of each chapter. As a southern, white, evangelical Protestant of Scottish descent and orthodox Presbyterian theology, I have found some things in their writings hard to understand, though I have genuinely tried. Perhaps there are also truths in my own heritage that they may have missed. The reader is challenged to judge these "prophets" by those whom the church's canon has always recognized as authentic.

This book is written on the assumption that most of its readers are, like its author, of a complacent and privileged class. It is hard for us to open our hearts and minds to the thought that God may be raising up new prophets to denounce us for the injustices we condone. My plea is that you will listen to these four Christians with the thought that they just may be saying things we desperately need to hear.

Yet, if they prick our consciences and even grieve us with their reminders of the misery of so many in our world, they also have another message. They are all theologians of hope. The good news of the gospel is that God's kingdom is coming. If we are at work in the cause of justice and freedom, we can live in a glorious faith. We have the assurance of Christ that in the end, in spite of all appearances to the contrary, we shall find that we have been on the winning side.

Study Suggestions

1. *Four Modern Prophets* proposes a controversial idea. It suggests that we have genuine prophets in the church today, men and women who are in some sense comparable to the prophets in the Bible. That proposal itself immediately raises two questions:
(a) Do you believe that God does in fact continue to raise up prophets now just as in Bible times? yes __ or no __
(Or maybe you have an answer which is not quite either one of those.) Why do you answer as you do? If you are studying with a group, compare your answer with those of the others.
(b) Whichever way you answered, what exactly do you mean by the word "prophet"? Try writing out your definition and, again, if you are in a group, compare your answer with those of the others.

2. Many would define a prophet as *one who predicts the future.* Biblical prophets certainly did provide us inspiring visions of what God intends for us. Make a note of what seem to you to be the most important ideas in the visions of a glorious future described in such prophetic passages as the following:

   > Isaiah 2:4; 11:1–9
   > Jeremiah 33:14–15
   > Ezekiel 34:25–31
   > Hosea 2:16–20
   > Zechariah 9:9–10

3. A broader definition of the word "prophet," however, might be *one who speaks forth for God,* especially the message of justice for all. Often the prophets' predictions of the future were

warnings that disaster would follow if certain groups were neglected. See how that understanding of the nature of prophecy is supported by the following passages and make a list of the groups whose cause the biblical prophets championed:

Isaiah 1:11–17
Jeremiah 7:1–7
Ezekiel 22:6–15
Amos 2:6–7; 5:10–13, 21–24
Micah 6:8
Malachi 3:5

4. Note now that there were prophets in the New Testament church. See such verses as:

Acts 13:1; 21:9
1 Corinthians 12:28
Ephesians 4:11

5. In reviewing the biblical prophets it may be wise to remember that they were not always popular in their own day. Recall, for example, what happened to one of the prophets as indicated in Jeremiah 20:1–2; 26:8; 32:2–3; 37:15; and 38:6. Note how Jesus summarized the reception God's people have typically given their prophets (Matt. 23:37).

6. Having reviewed all of these Bible passages above, try now to answer these questions relating to the possibility of prophecy in our own day:

(a) If there were a prophet today, what kinds of things do you think she or he would be preaching to us?

(b) Can you in fact name anyone in modern times whom you do regard as like the biblical prophets?

(c) What about the ministry of your own congregation? Is it "prophetic" in its concern for the oppressed people whose cause the biblical prophets—and the four described in this book—have championed?

1

Walter Rauschenbusch
and the Social Gospel

"Repent, for the kingdom of heaven is at hand."
(Matthew 4:17)

"Walter, what are you going to be when you grow up?"

"John the Baptist," the young Rauschenbusch replied.

More nearly than most of us, perhaps, Walter Rauschenbusch fulfilled his childhood ambition: he devoted his life to heralding the kingdom of God.

By Walter Rauschenbusch's definition of a prophet, he himself, though he might not have admitted it, was prophetic. Here is how he described the biblical prophets:

> These men were so alive to God and felt his righteousness so overpoweringly that they beat their naked hands against jagged

9

injustice and inhumanity. They were centers of religious unrest, creators of a divine dissatisfaction, and the unsparing critics of all who oppressed and corrupted the people.

The prophets were religious reformers demanding social action. They were not discussing holiness in the abstract, but dealt with concrete, present-day situations in the life of the people which were sometimes due to the faults of the people themselves, but usually to the sins of the ruling classes. They demanded neighborly good will and humane care of the helpless. But their most persistent and categorical demand was that the men in power should quit their extortion and judicial graft. . . . They all had a radiant hope of a future when their social and religious ideals would be realized.[1]

That was a kind of unconscious self-portrait by Walter Rauschenbusch. Let me present him now as a twentieth-century prophet.

Here is one sign of how effective a prophet Rauschenbusch turned out to be. Most of us have heard the phrase "the social gospel." You may have heard it denounced as the work of the devil, but you have heard of it. It was not the invention of Satan. The one who popularized the phrase and developed its theology and, for better or for worse, made "the social gospel" part of American Christianity was the prophet of whom we are speaking, Walter Rauschenbusch. Probably more than any other single individual of his time he changed the nature of mainline American Protestantism.

To the life and thought of this "prophet," therefore, we turn now.

Life and Early Influences

If throughout his life Rauschenbusch was concerned for the plight of American immigrants, it was in part because his family had once been among them. Just fifteen years before Walter was born, his father had left Germany for America. When Walter was born in 1861, thousands of German immigrants were pouring into the New World to live in its tenements, work in its sweatshops, or join the lines of its unemployed. Walter's father, however, was a minister, a former Lutheran turned Baptist, who became a professor at the seminary in Rochester, New York. It was there that Walter grew up.

There is a saying that "preachers' kids always turn out bad." Walter wrote later that in his teens he seemed to be headed that way, trying to outdo the other boys in swearing and other kinds of adolescent mischief. Soon, however, he had a genuine conversion experience. He wrote of it:

> And then, physically, came the time of awakening for me . . . and what I said to myself was: "I want to become a man; I want to be respected; and if I go on like this I cannot have the respect of men." This was my way of saying "I am out in a far country and I want to get home to my country and I do not want to tend hogs any longer," and so, I came to my Father, and I began to pray for help and got it; and I got my own religious experience.[2]

He never repudiated that religious conversion, but he did recognize later that it was incomplete.

> Such as it was, it was of everlasting value to me. It turned me permanently and I thank God with all my heart for it. It was a tender, mysterious experience. It influenced my soul down to its depths. Yet, there was a great deal in it that was not really true.[3]

What it lacked, he came to realize, was a conversion away from the sins which affect our social life and a conversion toward the building of a better world.

Having been thus far converted, he spent four years of study back in his second homeland, Germany. A brilliant student, he wrote letters home in Latin and Greek. After returning to this country, he attended the University of Rochester and then Rochester Theological Seminary. He spent two summers as student pastor of a little church in Kentucky. Upon graduation he almost went to India as a missionary. Instead he went, as a different kind of missionary, to New York City. He became pastor, at six hundred dollars per year, of a congregation of one hundred and forty-three German working-class Baptists, not far from the edge of a slum called Hell's Kitchen.

Rauschenbusch's social concern was not developed in his university study of Hegelian philosophy; it was prepared in the city. Later he wrote of those days with his immigrant congregation.

For eleven years I was pastor among the working people on the West Side of New York City. I shared their life as well as I then knew, and used up the early strength of my life in their service. . . . If this book in some far-off way helps to ease the pressure that bears them down and increases the forces that bear them up, I shall meet the Master of my life with better confidence.[4]

He got to know women so underpaid in their factory jobs that they had to walk the streets every night as prostitutes. He told of an old man he knew who was hit by a streetcar. When the old man could not pay for his medical care, he was ejected from the nearby hospital and taken in the middle of the night by boat to a charity hospital. It was so crowded that, when at last the old man's wife found him, he was out in the hall. That was all right, the authorities assured her, since there was nothing seriously wrong with him. Gangrene set in, however, and soon he was dead. The streetcar company settled with the wife for one hundred dollars. After all, they said, he wasn't earning much in the first place and was so old he wouldn't even make that small amount much longer. The widow had no choice but to accept the hundred-dollar settlement. Hence, it was not from an ethics class that his passion for social reform developed. He wrote:

It came from outside. It came through personal contact with poverty, and when I saw how men toiled all their life long, hard, toilsome lives, and at the end had almost nothing to show for it; how strong men begged for work and could not get it in hard times; how little children died—oh, the children's funerals! They gripped my heart.[5]

He also saw "good" Christians who were "born again" but who were not concerned. It bothered Rauschenbusch that so many, who like himself had had genuine, individual, personal conversions, still lacked any sense of social sin.

In seminary Rauschenbusch had become convinced that his mission in life was to "preach the gospel and save souls," bringing individuals to salvation in the most traditional and pietistic sense. After being among working people, however, he became disturbed by a new sense of the nature of human sin. Drinking, dancing, and card-playing were the favorite sins for some ministers to denounce, but Rauschenbusch felt a call instead to minister to the victims of *social indifference, political corruption,* and *economic greed.* It shook him that the slum landlords and the sweatshop owners were often sincere Christians, faithfully worshiping in fashionable churches while around them slum children were dying of malnutrition and the diseases poverty brings.

As far as an intellectual grasp of social problems was concerned, Rauschenbusch later wrote that he owed his first awakening to the "agitation" of Henry George.

Henry George—that name is scarcely a household word today. George's scheme of a "single tax" was abandoned long ago, but this colorful little man with the Buffalo-Bill-style moustache and goatee was once so popular that he beat Teddy Roosevelt in a race for mayor of New York. (Ironically the candidate of the corrupt Tammany machine beat both of these progressives!) Henry George was a school dropout at thirteen, put to sea for India, acquired a pet monkey, finally jumped ship in California, prospected there for gold, and failed. Unable to find a job and with his wife on the verge of having a baby, George became so desperate that he stopped a man on the street and begged for five dollars. "If he had not given it to me I think I might have killed him," George later wrote. Fortunately, he got the money and then a job with a newspaper, and eventually he became world-famous for his writings on poverty and his prescription for its cure.

What Rauschenbusch got from George, however, was not so much George's cure-all, the scheme of the "single tax," as it was his vision of what modern society could become.

> With want destroyed; with greed changed to noble passions; with the fraternity that is born of equality taking the place of the jealousy and fear that now array men against each other . . . who shall measure the heights to which our civilization may soar? Words fail the thought! It is the Golden Age . . . ![6]

Words did not fail Walter Rauschenbusch. He knew the name of that golden age. The Bible, Rauschenbusch was sure, means that age when it speaks of *the kingdom of God.*

The Kingdom of God

Rauschenbusch, we have seen, had been reared on personal conversion and piety and had been devoted initially simply to preaching and saving individuals. After being near Hell's Kitchen and in other areas of poverty, he was faced with the results of social sin and became aware of a new vision of social order. He admitted that at first he just did not know how to put these two together—traditional biblical piety and his new social concern. He wrote:

> And then the idea of the Kingdom of God offered itself as the real solution for that problem. Here was a religious conception that embraced it all. Here was something so big that absolutely nothing that interested me was excluded from it. Was it a matter of personal religion? Why the Kingdom of God *begins* with that! The powers of the Kingdom of God well up in the individual soul; that is where they are born, and that is where the starting point must necessarily be. Was it a matter of world-wide missions? Why that *is* the Kingdom of God, isn't it?—carrying it out to the boundaries of the earth. Was it a matter of getting justice for the working man? Is not justice a part of the Kingdom of God? Does not the Kingdom of God consist simply of this—that God's will shall be done on earth, even as it is now in heaven? And so, wherever I touched, there was the Kingdom of God.[7]

He said that the realization that the kingdom of God is central came to him like a revelation, like the peak of a mountain suddenly breaking through the clouds.

> It responded to all the old and all the new elements of my religious life. The saving of the lost, the teaching of the young, the pastoral care of the poor and frail, the quickening of starved intellects, the study of the Bible, church union, political reform, the reorganization of the industrial system, international peace,—it was all covered by the one aim of the Reign of God on earth.[8]

The key to understanding the Christian life, for him, was not just the personal religious experience, not just looking for the second coming some day, not just the imitation of Christ or practicing the Golden Rule, helpful as they are. Rather, it was the life devoted to the reign of God on earth, in individual hearts and in all society.

The Kingdom of God is the first and most essential dogma of the Christian faith. It is also the lost social ideal of Christendom. No man is a Christian in the full sense of the original discipleship until he has made the Kingdom of God the controlling purpose of his life.[9]

Biblical Basis

Rauschenbusch was sure that he had not invented this idea. Dedication to the kingdom as the ideal social order seemed to him to be the unifying theme of the whole Bible, but it was especially the theme of his two favorite parts of Scripture: the Old Testament prophets and the Synoptic Gospels' picture of the teachings of Jesus.

The prophets, he said, are "the beating heart of the Old Testament." This was not, however, because they gazed into crystal balls and predicted some future coming of Jesus. It was because they demanded, "Let justice roll down like waters, and righteousness like an ever-flowing stream" (Amos 5:24). They did not call for ceremony. "What does the Lord require of you but to do justice?" (Mic. 6:8). They preached the rule of God, a theocracy, and that meant, "the complete penetration of the national life by religious morality. It meant politics in the name of God."[10] They were religious reformers demanding social action. They were "radicals." They were "revolutionists." "And in Jesus and the primitive Church the prophetic spirit rose from the dead."

"Jesus was not a social reformer in the modern sense." Rauschenbusch knew that, and he wrote that if all the social reforms ever dreamed of were accomplished there would still be empty souls needing what only true religion can offer. Jesus spoke and thought strictly in religious terms, but he was the heir of the prophets, preaching their condemnation of sin and their love of even the poorest. He was the "initiator of the Kingdom of God."

"Repent, for the kingdom of heaven is at hand" (Matt. 3:2; 4:17). So the Gospels summarize Jesus' message, Rauschenbusch pointed out. What, then, did Jesus mean by "the kingdom of God"? Whatever else that phrase meant, Jesus would not have used it if it did not mean something of what his Jewish hearers had always understood it to mean. It involved the social justice which the law of Moses had prescribed and which the prophets had preached. Jesus was no sociologist, but he was one who preached against sin: the neglect of the poor by the rich, living for money, lack of concern for the sick, indifference toward those in prison. Jesus, it is true, revised the idea of the kingdom. It would not come by violence but by growth. It would break out of national and racial boundaries to reach the whole world. It was not just for a remote future. It was God's will being done here and now. He taught his disciples to pray for the kingdom as God's will being done *on earth* as it is in heaven. It was the kingdom of God because it was the kingdom of *love*, "a society-making quality." Jesus perfected the idea of the kingdom, but it was still the kingdom of the one of whom Mary sang as she awaited Jesus' birth:

> he has put down the mighty from their thrones,
> and exalted those of low degree;
> he has filled the hungry with good things,
> and the rich he has sent empty away.
>   (Luke 1:52–53)

Crusading for the Kingdom

Having been converted not just to a lonely individual piety but to social concern, our new "John the Baptist" set out to preach and work for the kingdom.

One of his first acts was to gather a group of like-minded souls who banded together to form what they called "The Brotherhood of the Kingdom." That fellowship grew and flourished. Rauschenbusch also became founder and editor of a periodical called *For the Right*. It was never highly successful financially or in number of subscribers, but *For the Right* did give Rauschenbusch a chance to present his new ideas to hundreds of others who began to agree.

Hard work in the pastorate began to wear down his health. In 1888 the Russian grippe left him tragically hard of hearing. The year before, he had turned down the offer of a position at Rochester Theological Seminary, rejecting the ivory tower of a professorship for work among the common people. During his eleven years as a pastor his congregation grew in membership from one hundred and forty-three to some two hundred and ten. His deafness, however, more and more handicapped his work in the pastorate. Therefore in 1897 he accepted a renewed call from the seminary, determined to teach the social gospel to a new generation of ministers.

He was, his students report, an excellent teacher. Rauschenbusch's impact on the country, however, did not come primarily from his students; it came from his pen. In 1907, at the age of forty-six, he published his first book, *Christianity and the Social Crisis*. It was, he later wrote, a "dangerous book." It was full of what he was willing to admit were "radical" ideas. As soon as it was published he went back to Germany for a year of graduate study, frightened that when he got back to America he might find that he had lost his job. Instead, to his surprise, he returned to find that his book had been an almost instant success. He was quickly called upon to address a distinguished audience of some five hundred in New York City. President Roosevelt consulted him about social policy. Everywhere people begged him to come and speak. There were those who attacked his social gospel as heresy, of course, but even they helped make his ideas known. He was a man with the right message at the right time. The early 1900s were a time of transition, of new social concern—labor unions were being born, antitrust laws were being passed, prohibition was a popular cause, minimum wage laws were being advocated—and Rauschenbusch was able to present a biblical basis for the best social movements of the era.

Christianizing the Social Order was published in 1912. It outlined specific proposals for achieving the kingdom. Much as the prophets of old had done, Rauschenbusch denounced a religion of worship though not one of works, but his *Prayers of the Social Awakening* taught thousands to pray in ways that expressed the new social concern. Literally hundreds of thousands of other words of Rauschenbusch appeared in print, but perhaps the most effective of his works was the book published in 1917, just a year before his death in 1918. Its title contained the phrase so closely associated with Rauschenbusch, *A Theology for the Social Gospel*.

The Doctrines of the Social Gospel

If you want an easily read introduction to Rauschenbusch, *A Theology for the Social Gospel* may be the best place to start. It goes through the traditional doctrines of the Christian creeds and reinterprets them in the light of his understanding of the Bible's social concern. It is natural, therefore, that the book begins not with the doctrine of God the Creator but with the *doctrine of sin*. What Rauschenbusch tried to do was to expand our consciousness of sin so as to make us aware of those social ills which, he was sure, the church has so often ignored.

He included this delightful story. In Toronto it was the practice that if milk were found to be contaminated it was poured out and the cans were marked with red paint. Thus the farmer who brought tainted milk was exposed to ridicule by the other farmers. One man found his milk thus wasted and his cans marked red. He became so angry that in spite of his religious scruples he began loudly to curse and swear. He was hauled up before his church and censured. The point of the story is that what his church condemned him for was cursing and swearing. The fact that he was introducing cow dung into the stomachs of little children was not mentioned at all.

Rauschenbusch quoted a New York minister as having said that there are four sins from which a Christian must abstain: drinking, card-playing, dancing, and going to movies. Rauschenbusch, by contrast, defined sin as selfishness. "We rarely sin against God alone." We sin against other people.

> To find the climax of sin we must not linger over a man who swears, or sneers at religion, or denies the mystery of the trinity, but put our hands on social groups who have turned the patrimony of a nation into the private property of a small class, or have left the peasant labourers cowed, degraded, demoralized, and without rights in the land.[11]

Christians have always said that it is a sin to murder someone with a knife, but Rauschenbusch wrote that it is possible to kill a child just as surely with a tenement as with a stiletto. The sins to be denounced are ours, such as when we fail to enact fair housing laws or laws to regulate factories, or the sins of those whose stock market panics when there is a rumor that peace may be coming. Sin as selfishness could be seen, he felt, in a whole economic system which is built on the profit motive, on greed.

Salvation, too, must be reinterpreted in social terms. Rauschenbusch did not want to do away with individual salvation, of course, but he wrote:

> Some who have been saved and perhaps reconsecrated a number of times are worth no more to the Kingdom of God than they were before. Some become worse through their revival experiences, more self-righteous, more opinionated, more steeped in unrealities. . . . If sin is selfishness, salvation must be a change which turns a man from self to God and humanity.[12]

Conversion must occur for superpersonal forces, too. Dictatorships must be changed into democracies. Economic systems must be changed from fostering greed to encouraging cooperation and compassion.

The church is "the social factor in salvation." Its function is to bring social forces to bear on social evils. Yet the church must never be confused with the kingdom of God, an error which has characterized too much of church history. Too often the church, proud of its own importance, has been a conservative force on the side of the rich. "The institutions of the Church, its activities, its worship, and its theology must in the long run be tested by its effectiveness in creating the Kingdom of God."[13]

Jesus Christ is "the Initiator of the Kingdom of God." For too long, Rauschenbusch felt, the church had wasted its time in metaphysical debates about the nature of Christ, about what is meant by saying that he was "God incarnate." "The social gospel wants to see a personality able to win hearts, dominate situations, able to bind men in loyalty and make them think like himself, and to set revolutionary social forces in motion."[14] It was Jesus' character, not his metaphysical nature, which mattered. It was not some supernatural birth but his personality which set humans to work for the kingdom.

> So we have in Jesus a perfect religious personality, a spiritual life completely filled by the realization of a God who is love. All his mind was set on God and one with him. Consequently it was also absorbed in the fundamental purpose of God, the Kingdom of God.[15]

Jesus' atoning death, therefore, is not to be understood in terms of medieval theories of the atonement. Rather we can best understand it when we realize that Jesus was killed by the forces of the corporate sins of his day. Rauschenbusch discussed in succession how each of the following sins contributed to Jesus' death: religious bigotry, graft and political power, corruption of justice, mob spirit and mob action, militarism, and class contempt. Jesus died fighting these, and his death is redemptive because it reveals those sins in all their horror, sets perfect love over against them, and summons us now to the prophetic mission of working against them for the kingdom of God.

Finally, *eschatology* does not center on some future coming of the kingdom, beyond history, at the end of time. "The Kingdom of God is humanity organized according to the will of God."[16] We are not to stand with the millennialists gazing into heaven. We are to share in the process of the evolution of that kingdom here and now.

His Advocacy of Economic Reforms

All of this theology pointed Rauschenbusch to many specific ethical concerns, but for this child of German immigrants the most pressing specific need was the gradual reform of the economic system. He had watched the people laboring near Hell's Kitchen, and he wrote scathingly of those who wanted no modification of free enterprise:

> Imagine a man who has been out of work for six weeks. His baby is sick, his credit at the grocery exhausted. He has stood in line with fifty other men, and his heart is in his throat when the foreman passes him in. He may not know that eleven hours are a day's work in this shop, and that skilled hands rarely make more than $9.20 a week. He would take the job on almost any terms; he has to. But the law calls this procedure a contract, and it protects the man's "liberty" to take as low a wage as he wants. . . . We cannot afford to have bright-eyed children transformed into lean, sallow, tired, hopeless, stupid, and vicious young people, simply to enable some group of stockholders to earn 10 per cent.[17]

When a New York minister called for guns to put a stop to a strike, Rauschenbusch wrote a scathing reply: "when have the police ever been used to stop the exploitation of labor by the supposedly Christian factory owners?" Hence Rauschenbusch championed what he called "Socialism," though it was not a doctrinaire but a Christian socialism. He did so aware that he would be accused of "atheism, free love, and red-handed violence," all three of which, of course, he denounced as strongly as he did the capitalism of his day.

It shocks many of us to see this good Baptist preacher preaching socialism. Advocate it he did, however, repeatedly. Capitalism, he maintained, was a system based on the profit motive, that is, on the desire for selfish gain, and to Rauschenbusch selfishness was sin. He never equated the socialist state with the kingdom of God, but, if that kingdom meant humankind organized according to God's will, then the kingdom's economic system could scarcely be based on the sinful quest for selfish profit.

Rauschenbusch knew the arguments in favor of capitalism. He admitted that "CAPITALISM is the most efficient system for the creation of material wealth which the world has ever seen."[18] To him, however, justice was more important than wealth. He knew, too, the argument that "Socialists" and "Labor Unionists" wanted pay without having to work. He wrote:

> We have been told that in one of the institutions on Blackwell's Island this sign has been put up: "It is a bad day for a young man when he first gets the idea that he can get a dollar without doing a dollar's worth of work for it." Amen! It is a good motto in the proper place. Now will not some lover of men have a few hundred mottoes painted with these words: "It is a bad day for a young man when he first gets the idea that he can get a million dollars without doing a million dollars' worth of work for it." Then let him distribute the signs downtown where they will do the most good.[19]

Those unearned millions were characteristic of capitalism as he saw it, and his heart anguished over the condition of those whose work really produced those millions hoarded by the rich.

Having said that he called himself a socialist and attacked capitalism, let us note some cautions. The capitalism he attacked was the unrestrained capitalism of the turn of the century. Things we now take for granted, partially because of Rauschenbusch's influence, are at least part of what he meant by "Socialist" reforms. In those days there were no minimum wage laws. Children were enslaved in sweatshops. Women got lower pay than men. Health and safety precautions hardly existed. People worked ten and twelve hours a day, and at near starvation wages. What Rauschenbusch crusaded for was the improvement of the lot of working people, not a doctrinaire program. Rauschenbusch, in fact, never joined the socialist party. He could be almost as critical when talking to a socialist audience as he was when writing for his usual capitalist readers. He criticized socialists for being materialists, often atheists, rigid dogmatists, and intent on violent revolution.

Theodore Roosevelt asked Rauschenbusch's advice about social programs, and Rauschenbusch recommended socialism. "Not while I'm president," said Mr. Roosevelt. "I am going to take what is good in Socialism and leave out the bad." "If you can really include what is good in it, fine," Rauschenbusch readily agreed.

Rauschenbusch feared that violence might come and implied that Christians might have to accept it. Far from advocating the communists' violent revolution, however, Rauschenbusch advocated reform-after-reform evolution. He wanted a minimum wage, restriction on the number of hours women and children could be made to work, old-age pensions, better health care, a graduated income tax, public ownership of public utilities, and the abolition of any system which allowed the rich to get richer through war.

Prophetic Predictions

We began by calling Walter Rauschenbusch a "prophet." One thing prophets are supposed to do is to prophesy or predict the future. Rauschenbusch would be the first to protest, of course, by saying that the prophets were primarily concerned to attack the social ills of their own day, not to engage in long-range speculations about distant events. Nevertheless, Amos, Isaiah, Jeremiah, and the rest did make predictions. Rauschenbusch, too, as a herald of the kingdom of God talked about events to come.

Liberal theology, of which Rauschenbusch was surely an adherent, has often been accused of a naïve optimism. Certainly one can find passages in the writings of Rauschenbusch which seem to exude a buoyant hope. "The kingdom of heaven is at hand," John the Baptist and Rauschenbusch preached, and Rauschenbusch seems to have had no doubt that some kind of socialism was coming. In this, of course, history proved him remarkably correct. A generation after his death Russia and China—more than a quarter of the world—were communist, the Scandinavian countries and Great Britain were at least moderately socialist, and in this country a second President Roosevelt had inaugurated many of the "Socialist" reforms for which Rauschenbusch had crusaded.

Yet Rauschenbusch was no naïve optimist. The careful reader of Isaiah, Jeremiah, and the other great biblical prophets of social justice will note that they so often presented their forecasts in conditional terms. Note the *if's* in Jeremiah's Temple Sermon:

> "For if you truly amend your ways and your doings, if you truly execute justice one with another, if you do not oppress the alien, the fatherless or the widow, or shed innocent blood in this place, and if you do not go after other gods to your own hurt, then I will let you dwell in this place." (Jer. 7:5–7)

Though he did preach with faith, there is, in Rauschenbusch's glowing pictures of the future, the same kind of caution found in Jeremiah 7.

> Perhaps these nineteen centuries of Christian influence have been a long preliminary stage of growth, and now the flower and fruit are almost here. If at this juncture we can rally sufficient religious faith and moral strength to snap the bonds of evil and turn the present unparalleled economic and intellectual resources of humanity to the harmonious development of a true social life, the generations yet unborn will mark this as that great day of the Lord for which the ages waited, and count us blessed for sharing in the apostolate that proclaimed it.[20]

Our participation in that glorious future kingdom depends, he seems to say, on our commitment to social justice.

> I confess that my faith falters in the very act of professing it. The possibilities are so vast, so splendid, so far-reaching, so contradictory

of all historical precedents, that my hope may be doomed to failure. The American churches may write one more chapter in the long biography of the disappointed Christ, which our sons will read with shame and our enemies with scorn. But for the present the East is aflame with the day of Jehovah, and a thousand voices are calling. If failure comes, may it find our sword broken at the hilt.[21]

He was more certain that the reforms sought by the labor movement would come than he was that the church would take its proper place in guiding them. Could it be that the church in this country has failed to take its place in the midst of the labor movement? One of his predictions came true in frightful ways: he said that Christian idealism without social application was like a soul without a body but that socialism without religion would be like a body without a soul. In Joseph Stalin's Russia that soulless Frankenstein's monster became a reality; Rauschenbusch's warning was all too accurate.

Some Evaluative Comments

When Walter Rauschenbusch died in 1918, World War I was still at its bloodiest. Rauschenbusch had opposed American entry into the war, and he wrote that because of its horror he never expected to be quite happy again. That war, the Great Depression, and World War II disillusioned many liberals. It is now easy to point to faults in liberal theology. Karl Barth and Reinhold Niebuhr, among others, have done that for us. Niebuhr's students used to make fun of the liberals as worshipers of the great god "If Only. . . ." The liberal creed, they scoffed, was simply "What a great world this would be *if only* we would all try to be a little bit kinder." The Jesus who was seen primarily as the instigator of social reform tended to become a teacher of the trinity these students attributed to Unitarianism: "the fatherhood of God, the brotherhood of man, and the neighborhood of Boston." By contrast, they reminded us, the God Paul wrote about was a transcendent sovereign, not a partner with us in the struggle. Liberals lacked Paul's sense of the depth of human sin, they charged, and two world wars blasted away our optimism that the kingdom was about to evolve.

Perhaps one could say that what was wrong with the social gospel was that it was strong on the *social* but not strong enough on the *gospel:* it was close to being a salvation by works, presenting a noble ethic but not enough good news. Such a criticism should not be allowed to go completely unchallenged, however, and two of the many possible responses will be made here.

(1) However easy it may be to criticize the naïve liberalism of some of his less perceptive followers, Walter Rauschenbusch was by no means naïve. Long before Reinhold Niebuhr he was writing not only about individual sin but also about the larger powers which force us into sinful molds. He knew that if in any sense the kingdom did come it would involve God's activity, not just ours. He also wrote that if we ever did achieve a just state its citizens would still need the gospel. Perhaps this is why Reinhold Niebuhr, who, despite all his criticisms of liberal theology, was surely committed to social Christianity, could write that Rauschenbusch was "the real founder of social Christianity in this country" and was still "generally its most satisfying exponent."

(2) It may be true that Rauschenbusch's theology was lacking in a Pauline and transcendental dimension. Many of us know the truth of a more conservative and evangelical gospel. Traditional Christianity has put more emphasis on Christ on the cross. It sees him as the second person of the trinity, God actually giving God's own self for us sinful human beings. We know ourselves forgiven, saved by "amazing grace." This realization of the cross as the manifestation of such a transcendent love, however, ought not to make us any the less loving. Indeed this awareness has sometimes spurred humans to respond by giving their very lives in the fight for justice for all humankind.

Many of the reforms for which Walter Rauschenbusch fought have been achieved, but far too many still have not been. It may be that in our understanding of the Bible and theology subsequent thinkers have enabled us to go beyond Rauschenbusch, but in the battle against injustice God would be pleased indeed if any of us could come anywhere close to his commitment and effectiveness.

Study Suggestions

1. As a review of your study of the Introduction, compare what you found in your own Bible study about the prophets with what Walter Rauschenbusch found. What, if anything, does he add to what you found?

2. Which way do you understand the gospel:
   (a) as a call to personal, individual salvation and morality, as in much traditional Protestantism; or
   (b) as a call to action for social justice, bringing a hope for a better society; or
   (c) as both, as did Rauschenbusch?

3. Probably all true Christians sincerely want a society of peace and justice. Many Christians differ sharply, however, as to what the church should do to help achieve that goal. Which do you believe to be more effective?
   (a) The church should preach individual, one-by-one conversion and morality, believing that saved individuals will then transform society.
   (b) The church should also preach and work for legislation against such things as slums, sweatshops, war, etc.
   What led Rauschenbusch to the latter view?

4. Rauschenbusch believed that there are "born-again" Christians who are sincerely loving and devout in their private lives but who have never related their faith to such social and political concerns as the slums and the employment situations in their own communities. Can you think of any example of a similar contrast in your own life?

5. To Rauschenbusch the kingdom of God was "a religious conception that embraced it all," personal religion, missions, justice for the working person, political reform, and international peace. To see how basic the kingdom was to Jesus look at such passages as the following:
   —See the summary of Jesus' message according to Matthew 4:17, 23–24 and Mark 1:14–15. (Compare the message of John the Baptist in Matt. 3:2.)

—Note the promise with which the Sermon on the Mount begins (Matt. 5:3).

—Remember what Jesus said his followers must put first in life (Matt. 6:33).

—Recall the subject of almost all of Jesus' parables (Matt. 13:19, 24, 31, 33, 44, 47, 52, etc.).

—If you have time, using a concordance, look at the many, many other references to the kingdom in Jesus' teachings. Having looked at these verses, see if you can write out a brief summary of what you understand the kingdom to mean, what you pray for when you pray, "Thy kingdom come." If you are studying with others, compare your answer with theirs.

6. Now see what Rauschenbusch's understanding of the kingdom adds to what you have said.

7. Having envisioned the concept of the kingdom of God, Rauschenbusch set out to describe a theology in which this idea would be central. The Apostles' Creed, by contrast, though loved by millions, never mentions the kingdom. Indeed some people, noting that it goes directly from Jesus' birth to his death, have said that the most important thing—Jesus' life and teachings—is indicated in that creed only by a comma. What value, if any, do you think there was in Rauschenbusch's effort to write a new theology, *A Theology for the Social Gospel,* in which the kingdom would be central?

8. "Sin is selfishness." This is a starting point among Rauschenbusch's doctrines. What do you think of this definition? Is it
(a) too simple, leaving out some important ideas; or
(b) a needed correction to earlier, more complex definitions?

9. Try evaluating each of the doctrines described on pp. 18–20. What ideas does Rauschenbusch add which older creeds left out, and what ideas does he omit which seem important to you?

10. If your own denomination has adopted a statement of belief in the years following Rauschenbusch's work, you might examine it to see if it reflects the ideas he pioneered in advocating. Many twentieth-century creeds do!

11. Rauschenbusch advocated extensive economic reforms, even socialism. If you or the group with which you are studying

would like to explore that controversial idea further, you might get help from one of the books listed in the bibliography.

12. Rauschenbusch crusaded for the rights of labor, better housing, and world peace. If you are studying with a group, you might want to invite someone involved in working for one of these causes to present current needs and opportunities for service. A representative of a labor union, a welfare worker, or someone from a peace organization such as Clergy and Laity Concerned might help you think through what you could be doing to carry on some part of Rauschenbusch's work in your community.

2
Martin Luther King, Jr. and Civil Rights

"Do not resist one who is evil. But if any one strikes you on the right cheek, turn to him the other also. . . . Love your enemies and pray for those who persecute you." (Matthew 5:39, 44)

One day in the 1930s the pastor of a large Baptist church in Atlanta took his young son to a downtown shoe store. They sat in the first empty seats they came to and waited to be fitted.

"I'll be happy to wait on you if you'll just move to those seats in the rear," said the clerk politely.

"There's nothing wrong with these seats. We're quite comfortable here," the minister replied.

"Sorry," said the clerk, "but you'll have to move."

"We'll either buy shoes sitting here or we won't buy shoes at all," "Daddy" King retorted, and with young M. L. in tow he

29

marched out of the store. "I don't care how long I have to live with this system, I will never accept it," growled Martin Luther King, Sr. Years later the son, Martin Luther King, Jr., wrote that never before had he seen his father so angry.[1]

It was a miniature foretaste of the Montgomery bus boycott. Both father and son were to live to see such stores integrated. They were to see lunch counters, rest rooms, transportation facilities, and all public accommodations desegregated. Schools were integrated. Blacks were granted the right to vote. Job opportunities undreamed of before were available to Blacks. Martin Luther King, Jr. had had such a part in that transformation that he became *Time Magazine*'s "Man of the Year" and won the Nobel Peace Prize, and he had lived such a life that after his death he became the first American in a century to have an annual national holiday declared in his honor.

If a prophet is a herald of God's kingdom of love, justice, and unity, surely this Baptist preacher was among the greatest prophets this century has seen.

Early Life

As a Black child growing up in the depression, young M. L., as he was called, had ample opportunity to see firsthand those twin evils against which he was to fight: prejudice and poverty.

His first experience, though not his last, with a prejudiced law officer came when "Daddy" King was stopped for accidentally running a stop sign.

"All right, boy, pull over and let me see your license."

"I'm no boy," replied the senior King. Pointing to young Martin, he said, "This is a boy. I'm a man, and until you call me one, I will not listen to you."

The policeman was so shocked that he wrote up the ticket nervously and then rapidly rode away.[2]

M. L.'s best friends were two boys whose father ran a store across the street. The time came, however, when there was always some excuse for them not to be playing with him any more. Their mother was polite but she always gave some reason. Finally young

Martin's mother explained the real problem. "They are white, and you are Black. They don't want to associate with you any more." He rode in the back of the bus, attended a Black church, studied at a segregated school, and, if he had the money, went downtown to sit in a filthy gallery at the theater while the white folks enjoyed the movie in the good seats below.

He also saw poverty. Heads of families stood for hours in bread lines in that depression. At one time sixty-five percent of the Blacks in Atlanta were on relief. Young Martin, however, grew up in a home which was relatively secure financially. He also grew up very much in church—Sunday school, Training Union, Youth activities, the "Preacher's Kid."

A good student, he graduated from Morehouse College and in 1948 went north to Crozer Theological Seminary. He spoke with appreciation of the professors, the books, and the ideas he encountered there. The first one mentioned in his autobiographical *Stride Toward Freedom,* though, is the prophet of the social gospel. He wrote:

> I came early to Walter Rauschenbusch's *Christianity and the Social Crisis,* which left an indelible imprint on my thinking by giving me a theological basis for the social concern which had already grown up in me as a result of my early experiences. Of course there were points at which I differed with Rauschenbusch. I felt that he had fallen victim to the nineteenth-century "cult of inevitable progress" which led him to a superficial optimism concerning man's nature. Moreover, he came perilously close to identifying the Kingdom of God with a particular social and economic system. . . . But in spite of these shortcomings Rauschenbusch had done a great service for the Christian Church by insisting that the gospel deals with the whole man, not only his soul but his body; not only his spiritual well-being but his material well-being. It has been my conviction ever since reading Rauschenbusch that any religion which professes to be concerned about the souls of men and is not concerned about the social and economic conditions that scar the soul, is a spiritually moribund religion only waiting for the day to be buried.[3]

As he was completing his residency requirement for his doctorate at Boston University, two churches and three teaching positions were tentatively offered to him. He chose the smaller of the two churches, Dexter Avenue Baptist, in Montgomery, Alabama. As he prepared to preach a "trial sermon" there he resolved, "Keep Martin Luther King in the background and God in the foreground and everything will be all right. Remember you are a channel of the gospel and not the source."[4] The sermon was well received. He got the call, and in 1954, the year of the Supreme Court's historic decision for school integration, he began his ministry in what had been the first capital of the Confederate States of America.

In 1954 in Montgomery the median income for whites was $1,730 per year. For Blacks it was a little more than half as much, $970. Ninety-two percent of white people's homes had flush toilets but two-thirds of Black homes did not. The schools, transportation facilities, and all other public places were of course rigidly segregated, and, of the thirty thousand Blacks in Montgomery County of voting age, only two thousand had registered to vote.

As a pastor there, King joined the Black ministerial association, became involved with the NAACP, and met with the Council on Human Relations, in addition to working hard with his own congregation. He carefully prepared his sermons; he visited the sick; he visited in every home; and he reorganized the congregational structure. Under the new organization some were to work on finances, one committee was responsible for Christian Education, and another committee was to lead the church in social action. Perhaps the establishment of this latter committee was the first step in a new American revolution.

The Montgomery Bus Boycott

What precipitated the revolution, however, must have seemed at the time a minor incident. On December 1, 1955, Mrs. Rosa Parks, tired from work, sat down on the first seat she came to after passing the white section of a Montgomery city bus, but after the white section had filled she was ordered to stand so that whites could have her seat. She refused and was arrested.

E. D. Nixon, a leader in the NAACP, paid her bail money. Some influential women suggested to Nixon that he spearhead a boycott of the buses and he agreed. King offered his church as the location for a planning meeting. Forty people attended, the largest number of them being ministers. King agreed to have his church secretary mimeograph seven thousand leaflets advertising a mass meeting for the following Monday night. "DON'T RIDE THE BUS," the notice began; however, one Black woman who got a leaflet could not read. She got the white woman she worked for to read it to her. Her employer, in turn, called the newspaper, and soon the planners of the boycott had all the publicity they needed.

Monday morning, December 5, 1955, came. "Martin, Martin, come quickly!" his wife Coretta called. The first bus had passed by. "Darling, it's empty!" Soon another bus came and then another, and in those first three buses that morning there were only two passengers, both white. The boycott had begun. It was the beginning of a year-long battle against determined opposition, a battle which was finally to integrate Montgomery's public transportation.

That very afternoon King was elected to head a new organization, the Montgomery Improvement Association, and he was asked to speak at the mass rally planned for that night. Rushed here and there in efforts to help provide and coordinate transportation for the thousands of Blacks who usually rode the buses to work, King found himself with only twenty minutes to prepare to speak to the crowd which was overflowing the church and its parking lot. Exhausted and frightened, "with nothing left but faith . . . I turned to God in prayer . . . asking God to restore my balance and be with me."

It was that night, in his initial speech as a civil-rights leader, that King first enunciated the concept he had been working out, the idea to which he was to dedicate his life: his faith in the power of active, loving, nonviolent resistance.

Nonviolence

As a young pastor Rauschenbusch had worked out the problem of how to combine the individual piety on which he had been reared with the concern for social justice which his work in the slums forced upon him. King could build on that, but his was another problem: how could Blacks battle against oppression and yet act in Christian love for their oppressors? As he pushed his way through the crowd that Monday night in 1955 he thought:

> What could I say to keep them courageous and prepared for positive action and yet devoid of hate and resentment? . . . I would seek to arouse the group to action. . . . But I would balance this with a strong affirmation of the Christian doctrine of love.[5]

Thus he told them that there comes a time when people get tired—tired of being segregated and humiliated, of being kicked by the feet of oppression—but

> No white person will be taken from his home by a hooded Negro mob and brutally murdered. There will be no threats and intimidation. . . . Our method will be that of persuasion, not coercion. We will only say to the people, "Let your conscience be your guide." . . . our actions must be guided by the deepest principles of our Christian faith. Love must be our regulating ideal. . . . Love your enemies, bless them that curse you, and pray for them that despitefully use you.[6]

King then dedicated himself to keeping the movement going but in that loving, nonviolent way.

He got the idea of nonviolence from two sources: one was Jesus; the other was a Hindu called Mahatma Gandhi. When, years later, King visited India, he said that he might go to other places as a tourist but that he came to Gandhi's India as a pilgrim. While in seminary King had heard a lecture on Gandhi which he later described as "electrifying." He had immediately bought half a dozen books on Gandhi's life and works. It was the concept of *satyagraha* which so inspired the young theologue. Gandhi had said that, *satyagraha*, commonly translated as "passive resistance," might better be rendered "soul force." King called it "truth force" or "love force." By its use Gandhi and the thousands he led had persuaded the British at last to set India free. Gandhi himself found the roots of the idea not only in Hinduism but also in Jesus.

> It was the New Testament which really awakened me to the rightness and value of Passive Resistance.
> When I read in the Sermon on the Mount such passages as "Resist not him that is evil; but whosoever smiteth thee on thy right cheek, turn

to him the other also", and "Love your enemies; pray for them that persecute you, that ye may be sons of your Father which is in heaven", I was simply overjoyed. . . .

Passive Resistance is an all-sided sword . . . it blesses him who uses it, and also him against whom it is used, without drawing a drop of blood.[7]

King readily acknowledged his debt to his Hindu hero.

Gandhi was probably the first person in history to lift the love ethic of Jesus above mere interaction between individuals to a powerful and effective social force on a large scale. . . . I came to feel that this was the only morally and practically sound method open to oppressed people in their struggle for freedom.[8]

However, King also wrote:

It was the Sermon on the Mount, rather than a doctrine of passive resistance, that initially inspired the Negroes of Montgomery to dignified social action. It was Jesus of Nazareth that stirred the Negroes to protest with the creative weapon of love.[9]

Christ, King said, provided the motivation, but Gandhi taught them a great deal about techniques.

There is not enough room here to describe the complex, organized activities of the boycott: the cooperation of the Black taxi companies, the organization of car pools, the efforts at negotiation, the battles in court, the nightly pep rallies. The Blacks' demands were not great: they simply asked that Montgomery adopt the pattern already in use in Mobile, that Blacks would start filling up the bus from the back and whites from the front and the seats in the middle would go to whoever needed them first.

Resistance to this request, however, was adamant. At first the city council and the bus company simply issued statements of refusal and waited for the gradual decline of the boycott which, they were sure, the "niggers" could not maintain. Then they called a conference in which they got one old Black preacher to argue that the business of the church was simply to save souls, not to engage in social action. King replied that he and the others knew Christ the Savior, too, but they did not see that as an excuse to condone injustice.

Soon the opposition tactics got tougher. Threats on King's life began, by rumor, mail, and telephone. King pled with the others not to fight back with violence if he were killed. Then one night he got a telephone call, "Listen, nigger, we've taken all we want from you; before next week you'll be sorry you ever came to Montgomery."

King was very human. He was so frightened he could not sleep. Finally he prayed:

"I am here taking a stand for what I believe is right. But now I am afraid. The people are looking to me for leadership, and if I stand before them without strength and courage, they too will falter. I am at the end of my powers. I have nothing left. I've come to the point where I can't face it alone." At that moment [King later wrote] I experienced the presence of the Divine as I had never experienced Him before. [An inner voice seemed to say to him] "Stand up for righteousness, stand up for truth; and God will be at your side forever."[10]

On January 30, 1956, less than two months into the boycott, a bomb exploded on King's front porch, the first of many attempts on his life.

The city council used every quasi-legal means to break the boycott. Black drivers, including King, were arrested for alleged traffic violations. The Black taxi companies were forbidden to take passengers without the full fare. The car pools were declared illegal.

The Ku Klux Klan attempted to frighten the Blacks into submission. Hooded riders rode through the streets one night. The Blacks, however, simply turned on their lights, sat on their porches, and waved. Confused, the KKK nightriders turned and rode away. A second bomb appeared on King's porch, this time failing to explode. To everyone's surprise two whites were put on trial for this crime, but they were acquitted, even though they had signed confessions. Instead, King was arrested, tried, convicted of leading the boycott, and sentenced to pay a five-hundred-dollar fine. Hundreds of others were arrested on various charges. Throughout these events nearly all of the white ministers said nothing. Repeatedly King preached nonviolence, often stopping some criminal response just in time. "Love your enemies; bless them that curse you; pray for them that despitefully use you" was his theme. Still, he insisted, "Don't ride the buses!"

November 13, 1956, eleven months after the boycott began, at a moment when King was on trial again in a Montgomery courtroom, reporters brought the news. A federal court had ruled the Montgomery bus segregation laws were unconstitutional. On December 21 King and a white friend rode side by side in the front of a Montgomery bus! Within a week after the federal ruling whites rioted. The white ministerial association had refused even to issue a statement calling for courtesy. A teen-aged Black girl was beaten by four whites as she got off a bus. A pregnant woman was shot in the leg. Three churches and one minister's home were bombed. Night bus service was suspended. Yet it was soon clear that the battle was won. Bus service, now completely desegregated, returned to normal in Montgomery.

Birmingham

Certainly one reason for King's success was an invention of which Walter Rauschenbusch probably never dreamed, television. Through television the world watched as Montgomery Blacks took on the white power structure, suffered beatings and bombings, and won. When, after five years as pastor of Dexter Avenue Baptist Church in Montgomery, King returned to Atlanta to be his father's assistant at Ebenezer Baptist, he was known throughout the nation. Moreover, he was head of the Southern Christian Leadership Conference, which had chapters in dozens of cities working for civil rights.

Sometimes campaigns failed even with King as leader. A good example is the one at Albany, Georgia. There, in spite of months of demonstrations and jailings, the lunch counters remained segregated. Curiously, a nonviolent approach by the police seemed to make white resistance more effective. In spite of setbacks, though, the campaign in Albany did have one effect. Thousands of Blacks registered to vote, thus helping to elect the first governor of Georgia pledged to equal enforcement of the law.

One of King's most spectacular successes came in 1963 and was watched on television in every living room around the country: it was his effort to desegregate stores in downtown Birmingham.

King's motive was, in fact, a concern beyond Birmingham, a concern to catch the conscience of the whole nation. Alabama had just elected George Wallace as governor. At his inaugural he had loudly proclaimed, "Segregation now! Segregation tomorrow! Segregation forever!" King described Birmingham as the most segregated city in America. In the six years prior to King's 1963 demonstrations there had been seventeen unsolved bombings of Black churches or homes of civil-rights leaders in Birmingham. When the head of the local bus company sought to comply with the new federal laws by desegregating the bus station, he was arrested. One Black area was called "Dynamite Hill" because it had been bombed so frequently.

The local SCLC affiliate was headed by Fred Shuttlesworth, a Black minister. His children had been beaten with chains when they had attempted to enter a school; Shuttlesworth had been arrested eight times. He had, however, won promises from downtown merchants to desegregate rest rooms and water fountains, but the promises had not been kept. Presiding over the enforcement of segregation was Public Safety Commissioner Eugene (Bull) Conner. He was reported to have walked up and down city hall shouting, "Niggers and white folks ain't going to segregate together in this man's town!" As Shuttlesworth saw merchant after merchant going back on previously made promises, he called upon King to come and help. King recognized that Birmingham might be an ideal place to dramatize for the nation the struggle for integration.

On April 2, 1963, he flew to Birmingham and issued his first call to organize a sit-in. At first few people joined the campaign. It was decided, therefore, to enlist youth and even children as volunteers. In small groups these young people began to demand services in previously segregated lunch counters, drugstores, and downtown department stores. Within ten days four or five hundred Blacks had been arrested. Three hundred were crowded into jail in one day! On television the nation saw children marching up to the bared fangs of police dogs. Newspapers ran front-page pictures of Conner's police beating prostrate women. Fire hoses mowed down unarmed youths . . . and still they marched. Soon nine hundred children and young people had been arrested.

During the time of this unrest in Birmingham, King reported that a police officer asked a young girl participating in a demonstration what she wanted. She could not even speak plainly, yet she responded, "F'eedom."[11]

By May 6, 1963, three thousand Blacks were in jail. Yet the next day four thousand more paraded. Then there came the day when Conners gave the order and his own firefighters somehow could not turn their hoses on the praying, marching column again. At the same time, a careful check showed that only twenty Blacks shopped on a given day in all the downtown stores which were being boycotted.

One of those arrested, of course, was Martin Luther King. He had chosen April 12, Good Friday, as the appropriate day for his arrest. For more than twenty-four hours he was held in solitary confinement, forbidden access to a lawyer or even a visit from his wife Coretta. It was during this imprisonment that he penned on borrowed paper his famous "Letter from a Birmingham Jail" in response to a statement issued by some white ministers.

On April 12, 1963, eight white Birmingham clergy had issued a public statement expressing an understanding of the impatience of people who felt that their hopes were slow in being realized and also expressing confidence that negotiations could solve all problems. In the statement the demonstrations had been blamed on interference from the outside. The clergy had appealed to Blacks to discontinue participation and to put their trust in due legal process, and they had commended the law enforcement officials for their orderly carrying out of their duty.

History contains a number of important literary masterpieces coming from prison. One thinks immediately of Paul's prison epistles, Boethius' *The Consolations of Philosophy,* and Bunyan's *Pilgrim's Progress.* Martin Luther King's reply to the Birmingham clergy is in that tradition of literary masterpieces.[12]

He addressed his readers as "My Dear Fellow Clergymen." Since they had protested that the boycott was the result of outside interference he began by explaining that he was there by invitation from responsible Black leaders.

> But more basically, I am in Birmingham because injustice is here.
> Just as the prophets of the eighth century b.c. left their villages and
> carried their "thus saith the Lord" far beyond the boundaries of their
> home towns, and just as the Apostle Paul left his village of Tarsus and
> carried the gospel of Jesus Christ to the far corners of the
> Greco-Roman world, so am I occupied to carry the gospel of freedom
> beyond my own home town. Like Paul, I must constantly respond to
> the Macedonian call for aid. (page 78)

The clergy had called for patience. Perhaps that was easy for
them, King suggested. But they had never seen their fathers
humiliated by being called "boy" and "nigger," had never known
their mothers to be denied the title "Mrs.," and had never been
nagged by the ever present signs "white" and "colored." They had
not seen their loved ones beaten by white police, nor did they live
with twenty million brothers in a "cage of poverty."

The ministers were concerned, he noted, about the breaking of
laws. But he quoted to them the saying of St. Augustine that "an
unjust law is no law at all." The 1954 decision of the Supreme
Court, outlawing segregation, was the true law, for it was morally
right.

King now turned to the church. He, too, loved the church, he
reminded them. He had grown up in it, had devoted his life to its
ministry. But

> I have traveled the length and breadth of Alabama, Mississippi, and
> all the other southern states. On sweltering summer days and crisp
> autumn mornings I have looked at the South's beautiful churches with
> their lofty spires pointing heavenward. I have beheld the impressive
> outlines of her massive religious-education buildings. Over and over I
> have found myself asking: "What kind of people worship here? Who is
> their God? Where were their voices when the lips of Governor Barnett
> dripped with words of interposition and nullification? Where were they
> when Governor Wallace gave a clarion call for defiance and hatred?
> Where were their voices of support when bruised and weary Negro men
> and women decided to rise from the dark dungeons of complacency to
> the bright hills of creative protest?" (page 95)

He had wept over the church, King said, tears of love. But the
judgment of God, he warned these church leaders, was now upon

the church for its failure to stand for justice.
He concluded with

> If I have said anything in this letter that overstates the truth and
> indicates an unreasonable impatience, I beg you to forgive me. If I have
> said anything that understates the truth and indicates my having a
> patience that allows me to settle for anything less than brotherhood, I
> beg God to forgive me. (page 100)

He signed it, "Yours for the cause of Peace and Brotherhood, Martin Luther King, Jr."

In May 1963 an organization of one hundred and twenty five business leaders gave in to the Blacks' demands for desegregation and jobs. At his next press conference the president of the United States devoted his entire opening statement to Birmingham and civil rights. King and the Blacks had won.

Selma

Not all of King's campaigns ended in victory. In September of 1963 four young girls in a Birmingham Sunday school were dynamited to death by whites. At their funeral King still pled for nonviolence. Segregation was disappearing in many places, and King himself was now a world-renowned hero. His "I Have a Dream" speech on the steps of the Lincoln Memorial touched the hearts of millions. In December of 1964 he was awarded the Nobel Peace Prize.

The conviction was growing upon King that the best hope for Blacks to win justice nonviolently would be at the polls. He determined, therefore, to join with others who were working to give Blacks the ballot. He knew federal legislation would be required, but there was a need to dramatize the difficulties Blacks had in registering to vote. A clear confrontation might force a reluctant Congress and president to act. It was decided that the confrontation should begin in Selma, Alabama.[13]

In 1965 in Dallas County, where Selma is located, there were fifteen thousand Blacks. Of that number only three hundred and thirty-three were registered to vote. Every kind of legal and illegal tactic had been used to deny the Negro the franchise. Therefore, civil-rights groups began a series of marches on the courthouse of Dallas County. Repeatedly they were met with beatings and arrests.

Finally, on Sunday, March 5, 1965, five hundred marchers set out from Selma for Montgomery, the state capital, fifty miles away. At the bridge on the edge of town they were met by the county sheriff and Governor Wallace's state troopers. They were teargassed, beaten, shocked with electric cow prods, and chased back to their churches. Police seized one man and threw him bodily through a stained-glass window picturing Christ as the Good Shepherd. Of the five hundred marchers seventy were hospitalized and ninety others were treated for injuries.

The television cameras recorded it all. CBS interrupted the hit movie, *Trial at Nuremberg,* to show clips of the beatings. Protest marches sprang up all over the country. When King issued calls for additional marchers, especially from the clergy, Black and white church leaders poured in from all over America. One of them, Rev. James Reeb, a white Unitarian minister from Boston, was promptly murdered by white thugs in Selma. With the nation shocked, President Lyndon B. Johnson stood before TV cameras and a joint session of Congress, echoed King's ideas, demanded a strong voting rights act, and ended his speech, "And we *shall* overcome."

The march on Montgomery finally succeeded, protected by a court order. Twenty-five thousand people heard King speak again of his dream of racial unity, this time from the steps of the former capital of the Confederacy. On August 6, 1965, with King standing behind him, President Johnson signed the Voting Rights Act.

It was, biographer Stephen B. Oates says, King's finest hour.

Violence and Vietnam

The rest of the story is tragedy.

What probably distressed King most was that Blacks then began to turn to leaders who professed to offer a quicker solution to their problems: violence. The Black Muslims answered hate with hate.

The Student Nonviolent Coordinating Committee dropped the word "Nonviolent" from its title. Its new director, Stokely Carmichael, had gone almost crazy as he watched his followers being clubbed in Montgomery. "I started screaming and I didn't stop until they got me to the airport. That day I knew I could never be hit again without hitting back," Carmichael announced. He adopted a black panther as his symbol, and for King's slogan "Freedom Now!" he substituted "Black Power!" He fought against including any whites in his demonstrations. The chant went up, "Hey! Hey! Whattaya know! White people must go—must go!" "Jingle bells, shotgun shells, Freedom all the way, Oh what fun it is to blast, A trooper man away," marchers chorused.

Watts, a Black ghetto in Los Angeles, exploded in riots, burning, and looting. When King went to Chicago to speak to a Black audience, he was booed for the first time in his life. "I went home that night with an empty feeling," he later wrote. The nonviolence for which and by means of which he had fought so valiantly now seemed to be a lost cause, and with it, hope of further progress seemed to be vanishing. A long, bitter campaign in Chicago proved a failure. King and his family had moved into a slum there to share the conditions of the Chicago poor as they fought for open housing. All they won were promises, and the conviction grew on King that enforcement of open housing laws was not the key to eliminating bad housing anyway. Poverty must be removed. It did little good to tell Blacks they could legally move to the suburbs if they had no money to buy houses.

For years J. Edgar Hoover of the FBI had spread the lie that King was a tool of a communist conspiracy. Actually King had never had any admiration for the Russian dictatorship, but he did come more and more to agree with Rauschenbusch that economic justice demanded some modifications in any system which favored the greedy and neglected the needy. He began to plan that march on Washington which he would not live to see, "The Poor People's Campaign." Chicanos, native Americans, Appalachian whites, and poor Blacks were to walk across the south, invade the District of Columbia, and camp there until Congress came to their aid in the war on poverty.

King knew that the nation could not afford two wars at the same time, and an effective war on poverty required the end of the war in Vietnam. Vietnam was, he believed, a racist war. Only if the thirty billion dollars a year wasted fighting in Vietnam were to be rechanneled to restructure American economy could a just society be built. President Johnson, once King's supporter, was furious at what seemed to him betrayal. Others of King's followers felt he had betrayed them by associating civil rights with what was popularly regarded as an unpatriotic stance concerning the war.

Perhaps it was his growing concern about poverty which led him to accept an invitation to lead a demonstration in behalf of striking sanitation workers in Memphis, Tennessee. For months his followers had been worried about King's fits of deep depression, including his obsession with his impending death. Often he laughed about it; often he seemed to face it courageously; but sometimes he was clearly frightened, and so he spoke of his death in the speech he made the night before he died.

If God had given him a choice as to which century he would live in, King fantasized, he would not choose the days of Moses, the golden age of Greece, or even the Reformation. Instead he would select the twentieth century, for it was in this century that in South Africa, in Kenya, in Ghana, in New York, in Jackson, and in Memphis the cry had gone up, "We want to be free!" He had come to Memphis, King said, for the same reason the Good Samaritan had helped the man in need. He was aware, however, that he did so at risk to his own life.

> But it really doesn't matter with me now. . . . Because I've been to the mountaintop. . . . Like anybody I would like to live a long life. . . . But I'm not concerned about that now. I just want to do God's will. And He's allowed me to go up to the mountain. . . . And I've looked over. . . . And I've *seen* the Promised Land. . . . And I may not get there with you. . . . But I want you to know tonight that we as a people *will* get to the Promised Land. . . . With this faith, *we* will be able to achieve this new day, when all of God's children—black men and white men, Jews and Gentiles, Protestants and Catholics—will be able to join hands and sing with the Negroes in the spiritual of old, "Free at last! Free at last! Thank God Almighty we are free at last."[14]

The next day, April 4, 1968, an escaped convict, a white man, James Earl Ray, gunned down the prophet with one violent blast.

A Summary of King's Message

King was a preacher, an organizer, and a demonstrator, not a professor. Thus he left us no systematic theology to summarize his ideas. We can only select a few statements here and there for review and evaluation. Here are some obvious ones.

(1) He believed in the social gospel. Addressing Black ministers who were reluctant to march with him because they felt their place was simply to save souls, King protested that true religion

> seeks not only to integrate men with God but to integrate men with men and each man with himself. . . . Any religion that professes to be concerned with the souls of men and is not concerned with the slums that damn them, the economic conditions that strangle them, and the social conditions that cripple them . . . is the kind the Marxists like to see—an opiate of the people.[15]

(2) He believed in nonviolence and love. "When I speak of love, I am speaking of that force which all the great religions have seen as the supreme unifying principle of life. Love is the key that unlocks the door which leads to ultimate reality. . . . 'Let us love one another: for love is of God.'"[16] For King, turning the other cheek was essential to the Christian ethic. King's critics may legitimately question whether Jesus really intended nonviolence to be a technique by which the oppressed might gain justice. One may question whether that technique would be effective when used against people of a culture quite different from that of the British opponents of Gandhi or the southern whites of King. One cannot deny that King believed in it both as an end and as a means and that he achieved amazing results through love.

(3) Coupled with his belief in the power of active nonviolent resistance was a belief in the redemptive power of innocent suffering. That conviction consoled him concerning the persecution he and others experienced. Somehow, he believed, God would use undeserved suffering to bring reconciliation. He himself—if I have counted correctly—was arrested nineteen times. The FBI investi-

gated some fifty threats on his life. He was the object of repeated bombings. He frequently deliberately chose jail rather than bail or fine. He selected Good Friday as the day he would go to jail in Birmingham. "This," he said, "is the way of the cross." To King, Jesus' death was the supreme example of the redemptive power of suffering.

(4) He believed in the church and in its responsibility. Repeatedly he was disappointed: the white church in the south rarely supported his calls for justice. Yet he never completely gave up on the white church, and it was the Black church which made his mission possible.

> The church too must face its historic obligation in this crisis. . . . Racial segregation is a blatant denial of the unity which we have in Christ; for in Christ there is neither Jew nor Gentile, bond nor free, Negro nor white. Segregation scars the soul of the segregator and the segregated.[17]

He called upon the church to educate, to show the true aims of Blacks, thus calming the fears of whites to center its life on God, not custom, to take the lead in social reform, to desegregate itself, and to work for economic as well as racial justice.

(5) Finally, Martin Luther King, Jr. was a prophet in the traditional sense of the term. He was a man with an inspired vision of the future. There were times when he had confidence that the day of brotherhood would come soon. At that "finest hour" on the steps of the Alabama capital at the end of the march to Montgomery, King and the crowd almost chanted a chorus proclaiming the nearness of the day.

> How long? Not long, because no lie can live forever. How long? Not long, because you will reap what you sow. How long? Not long, because the arm of the moral universe is long but it bends toward justice. How long? Not long, cause mine eyes have seen the glory of the coming of the Lord. . . . *Glory, glory hallelujah!*[18]

At times he was very much like those biblical prophets who presented the future as conditioned upon the repentance of God's people. In his last book he wrote much less optimistically, "We still have a choice today: nonviolent coexistence or violent coannihilation. This may well be mankind's last chance to choose between chaos and community."[19]

In subsequent years, however, when people recalled King they particularly loved his glowing prophecy of the future in which he quoted the prophet Isaiah. His dream on the steps of the Lincoln Memorial is his best legacy to us.

I have a dream today.

I have a dream that one day the state of Alabama . . . will be transformed into a situation where little black boys and black girls will be able to join hands with little white boys and white girls and walk together as sisters and brothers.

I have a *dream* today . . . that one day every valley shall be exalted, every hill and mountain shall be made low . . . and the glory of the Lord shall be revealed, and all flesh shall see it together.[20]

Study Suggestions

1. Matthew 5:38–48 was a passage so basic to Martin Luther King, Jr.'s approach that the best way to begin study of this chapter is to review those verses. Do you think of them
   (a) as describing a way of action which is practical, which will "work"; or
   (b) as presenting an ideal we ought never to forget even though we cannot always follow it?
   King seems to have regarded these words as a very practical, workable guide.
2. Pp. 29–31 describe racial segregation which has been left behind in many ways in many places. If you are studying this book with others, there are probably older members of the group who can describe much the same conditions as those in which King was reared. Perhaps you can recall them, too. Even more important, can you or others point to conditions of this kind still very much with us today?
3. King describes how white clergy persuaded one Black preacher to try to argue with the leaders of the Montgomery boycott that the business of the church is to save souls, not to boycott businesses. How do you respond to King's reply? Which side do you think you and your church would have been on in that

dispute? Does the concern of the white churches not to get involved in a controversial crusade for justice seem to you a relic of that time and place, or is it typical of churches you know?

4. Have you or any in the group with which you may be studying had an experience you can tell about which is like King's sense of courage and support after the prayer he describes on pp. 35–36?

5. The text describes political conditions in the south in the early 1960s. There have been many changes since then, many of which are due to Martin Luther King, Jr. Can you list some of those changes? Do you know of political conditions in your community which are still like those which King fought? If so, what are they?

6. The letter from the Birmingham jail is probably the best known of King's writings. Review it now, reading the whole letter if you have access to it or at least the part reprinted here. It is, among other things, an indictment of the the white church as perceived by King. Do you think his criticisms were justified then? How involved in the struggle for justice is your church now?

7. You or your study group may know someone who was directly involved in the civil rights movement of the 1950s and 60s. If so you might ask that person to talk with you about the protests they saw which were like those in Birmingham and Selma.

8. If you are studying with a group you might get someone from the NAACP or the Urban League or some other group now at work for racial justice to talk with you about what still needs to be done in your community and how you and others can help.

9. As his movement grew, King had to fight for his pattern of nonviolence on two fronts. On the one front, he had to struggle to prevent the civil rights movement from falling into the hands of vengeful advocates of "Black power." On the other front, he had to take his stand against our national policy of violence in Vietnam. To what extent, if any, do you share King's view that our nation must both renounce military violence as a basis of

foreign policy and itself adopt as guidelines Jesus' words about turning the other cheek?

10. King was himself the victim of violence. His dream has not yet been fully achieved. Which of the following seems to you most nearly a correct evaluation of King's work?

   (a) In the end he was shown to have been too idealistic. He himself was killed, and his nonviolent approach never achieved all its goals. Violence is necessary.

   (b) He showed that nonviolent, loving work for justice wins out in spite of appearances to the contrary.

   (c) He showed that, though love is not necessarily a successful technique, it is the way worth dying for.

   (d) Something else, such as . . .

11. What do you and others think: will King's dream ever be realized?

12. Unlike the other "prophets" in this book, King never wrote systematically on theology. He was trained in theology, however, and pp. 44–47 summarize what seem to have been some major theological ideas of this thinker. They are rather different from what are found in most creeds. To what extent do they seem to you to be sound Christian doctrine, and where, if anywhere, do you think they may depart from orthodox Christianity?

3

Gustavo Gutiérrez
and Liberation Theology

"The Spirit of the Lord is upon me,
because he has anointed me to preach good news to the poor.
He has sent me to proclaim release to the captives . . .
to set at liberty those who are oppressed." (Luke 4:18)

On February 15, 1966, the Colombian army ambushed and shot to death the leader of a group of guerrilla revolutionaries. In itself there was nothing so very unusual about that: financed by our taxes, military dictatorships in Latin America repress, torture, and kill revolutionaries every day. Within two years, however, this particular revolutionist was hailed in posters and songs all over Latin America as a folk hero. What made him different was this: Camilo Torres was a Christian minister, a Roman Catholic priest.

Six months earlier Torres had temporarily ceased to function as a clergyman.

I have left the rights and privileges of the clergy but I have not ceased to be a priest. . . . I have stopped saying Mass in order to bring about love for neighbor in the temporal sphere, economic and social. When my neighbor has nothing against me, when I have brought about the Revolution, I will offer Mass again.

It is necessary, then to take the power away from the privileged minorities to give it to the poor majorities. This, if it is done rapidly, is the essence of a revolution. . . . The Revolution is the only way to get a government which feeds the hungry . . . not only occasionally and in passing, not only for a few but for the majority of our neighbors. For this reason the Revolution is not only permitted but obligatory for Christians who see in it the only efficacious way to bring about love for all.[1]

Even the often conservative Roman Catholic hierarchy soon heard echoes of Torres' protest. Two years after his death, meeting in Medellín, Colombia, a conference of Latin American bishops issued statements which included the following:

Poverty . . . is in itself evil. The prophets denounce it as contrary to the will of the Lord and most of the time as the fruit of the injustice and sin of men.[2]

God . . . sends his Son . . . so that He might come to liberate all men from the slavery to which sin has subjected them: hunger, misery, oppression and ignorance, in a word, that injustice and hatred which have their origin in human selfishness.[3]

These words, new for Latin American church officials, were proclaimed by Roman Catholic bishops, but behind the scenes was a Peruvian theology professor and activist who served as advisor at their conference. This man, who had helped to draft those statements about liberation and injustice, was an old friend of Camilo Torres from graduate school days. His name was Gustavo Gutiérrez. He is the best known spokesperson for liberation theology, probably the most influential movement in theology today.

It is to the life and thought of Gustavo Gutiérrez and to his liberation theology that we turn now.

Gutiérrez' Life

Gutiérrez was later to write of the "decisive influence" of Camilo Torres and of that other martyr to Latin American

revolution, "Ché" Guevara. It was not from the thought of any individuals, however, but out of a lifetime of identification with the poor that his understanding of liberation theology developed. To begin with, Gutiérrez was born part American Indian. Four centuries earlier the Indians had been conquered, baptized at the point of a gun, and then enslaved by their Spanish conquerors. Gutiérrez grew up among the poor.

Born in 1928 in Lima, Peru, his identification with the powerless was strengthened by a boyhood illness. Osteomyelitis kept him in bed for six years and left him with a permanent limp. He did, however, receive a good education. He studied medicine, planned to be a psychiatrist, and then decided instead to become a priest. An excellent student, he attended universities in the best Catholic pattern, in France and in Rome. A former professor says that, steeped in historical theology and philosophy, as a student Gutiérrez showed no particular interest in politics. When he returned to Peru to teach theology at the University of Lima, however, all that traditional classical education began to seem somehow irrelevant. It was in his encounter with the poor in the slums of that city that his liberation theology began to take shape.

There is horrible and extensive poverty in North America, but most of us belong to the relatively affluent middle class. Most people in Latin America, by contrast, are poor. In Peru in a recent year the inflation rate was one hundred and twenty percent. Sixty percent of Peruvians are underemployed or even unemployed. Hundreds of thousands have tea and bread for breakfast, soup, rice, and fruit or vegetable for supper, and that is all. Peru has a big fish cannery, but the much needed salmon does not go to the Peruvians. They cannot afford to buy it. It comes to North America. There have been efforts at industrial development following American patterns and with some American aid, but Gutiérrez discovered that, while in the sixties the developed nations increased their wealth by fifty percent, the "developing countries"—two-thirds of the world's population—continued in poverty. The gap between the rich and the poor became even greater.

All too often Latin American governments have been military

dictatorships kept in power in part by large contributions of United States aid. Their approach to the problem of poverty has been not so much to try to restructure an unjust economy as it has been to defend themselves militarily against what they perceive to be the "socialist-inspired" revolutions so ready to break out among the desperate. American tax dollars helped support the repressive dictatorship of Batista in Cuba until Castro overthrew it. The CIA and ITT united to help overthrow the democratically elected socialist government in Chile, and the military dictatorship in Brazil has received huge injections of United States financial support in spite of its torture of dissenters, including many priests. In recent months one hundred and twenty-four people in Peru have simply disappeared. Thousands are jailed without trial, and many are massacred.[4]

After young Gutiérrez returned to Latin America, he grew more and more horrified by this situation. One thing which particularly distressed him was the attitude of the church. Traditionally the church in Latin America has been on the side of the status quo and thus on the side of the rich against the poor. He traced its depressing history. Born in the days of the counter-Reformation, the Latin American church has always been conservative and defensive. It was brought to the New World by the Spanish conquerers who soon made up the rich elite. One of Gutiérrez' heroes is Bartolome de Las Casas, a bishop who pled the cause of the Indians during the Spanish conquests. Few paid attention, however, to that Christian. The church, Gutiérrez found, has usually been the bulwark of the rich against the struggles of the poor.

In the 1960s new things were beginning to happen. Vatican II brought a rising concern for the poor. More and more clergy began to speak in their behalf. Gutiérrez became particularly interested in the formation of *communidades de base*. These are grass-roots communities of sometimes fifteen to fifty people who share in Bible study, discussion of religion, teaching each other skills in farming or mechanics or even literacy, and political action, perhaps of a quite local nature. Some are led by priests; some are not. A hundred thousand have sprung up all over Latin America.

Gutiérrez decided not to live in Lima's pleasant university area. Instead he moved into the slums. His apartment is above the Bartolome de Las Casas Center, headquarters for his work among the poor. The first floor of the building is the store of a local merchant. "Abroad I'm regarded as a theologian," his friend Robert McAfee Brown reports Gutiérrez as saying, "but in Peru I'm thought of as an activitist."[5]

It was in 1973 when his book, *A Theology of Liberation*, was translated into English that Gutiérrez began to come to the attention of people in the United States. In 1975 he came to this country to address a conference of North and South American theologians called "Theology in the Americas—1975." The *Time* reporter who covered the conference described it as "curious."

> The participants would defend an argument with a scriptural passage from *Jeremiah* or a verse from *Luke*, then, just as earnestly, cite Marx in condemning economic injustice. The theology of liberation in fact combines Marxist economic analysis with the teachings of the Old Testament prophets and the commands of the Christian gospel to fashion a demanding spiritual ethic: that it is every Christian's duty to fight oppression, especially industrial capitalism, which is viewed by this theology as the central evil today.[6]

The *Time* reporter was right: this was "curious"! Hundreds of people from all over Latin America began to come to Gutiérrez' summer school lectures to learn more. Many of them were poor, some even illiterate. Two thousand came in a recent summer.

Ten years after his success at Medellín, angry conservatives excluded Gutiérrez from the 1979 conference of Latin American bishops, this time held at Puebla, Mexico. A preliminary paper, circulated for the bishops' consideration, was denounced by Gutiérrez as "tranquilizing." Not allowed into the conference hall, he and other theologians with liberation concerns rented a house nearby as the bishops were meeting. Between sessions they consulted with friends in the hierarchy. The conference ended with yet another strong statement concerning the need for economic transformation in behalf of the poor.

In 1983 the Vatican, somewhat alarmed by all this activity, sent a commission to investigate Gutiérrez' orthodoxy. Perhaps to its embarrassment, the commission was unable to propose a condemnation. Gutiérrez simply seemed not to have any theological heresies. He believed firmly in Christ as God incarnate, in the Bible as the Word of God, and in the Trinity. Accused by some of the materialism characteristic of Marxism, in 1983 he published *We Drink from Our Own Wells,* the entire volume being an exposition of the spiritual life which grows out of involvement with the poor and the suffering. Nevertheless investigation of his orthodoxy has taken so much of his time that he was unable to give his summer lectures in 1984. In September of 1984 network television in this country carried on the evening news the report of how the Sacred Congregation for the Doctrine of the Faith issued a strong statement condemning Marxism and by implication any liberation theology which might make use of it. Again, however, opponents of Gutiérrez were unable to substantiate charges of a "Marxist taint" in his writings.

Gutiérrez' first book was dedicated to Henrique Pereira Neto, a Black priest who had been assassinated. Another book included several quotations from Salvadoran bishop Oscar Romero, a more recent martyr. He also quoted Juan Alsina, another murdered priest. Although Peru is relatively less "repressive" than some other Latin American countries, people like Gutiérrez are always in danger of governmental action against them.

The Method of Liberation Theology

Let us turn now from the life of Gutiérrez to the nature of liberation theology.

Perhaps the most distinctive characteristic of liberation theology is not a certain set of doctrinal propositions but its perspective. Liberation theology is theology done from the point of view of the oppressed. Its content may vary depending on which group of the oppressed are doing it—the poor of the third world, Blacks in the United States, women, or other victims of oppression—but the various liberation theologies are all linked by that perspective. They grow out of involvement with people on the bottomside of life.

This means that to live from a liberation perspective you have to learn to read the Bible in a new way, quite likely the reverse of the way you have previously understood it. You need to listen to its words not as comfortably fixed persons hear them but as they sound to the poor. Try, for example, listening to these verses as though you were living in a tar-paper shack in a Mexico City slum and on the verge of starvation (these are all favorite texts of Gutiérrez);

> . . . the LORD has anointed me
> to bring good tidings to the afflicted;
> he has sent me to bind up the brokenhearted,
> to proclaim liberty to the captives,
> and the opening of the prison to those who are bound. (Isa. 61:1)

Thus says the LORD . . . "Let my people go." (Exod. 5:1)

> Father of the fatherless and protector of widows
> is God in his holy habitation. (Ps. 68:5)

> "Woe to him who builds his house by unrighteousness,
> and his upper rooms by injustice
> who makes his neighbor serve him for nothing,
> and does not give him his wages; . . .
> Did not your father eat and drink
> and do justice and righteousness?
> Then it was well with him.
> He judged the cause of the poor and needy;
> then it was well.
> Is not this to know me?
> says the LORD." (Jer. 22:13, 15–16)

The Hebrew Bible is the story of liberation. It tells how God liberated the Hebrews from their Egyptian masters. It tells how ever after they were to observe the Passover in order to celebrate that liberation. Their covenant demanded that in turn they were not to oppress anyone. After seven years their slaves were to be freed, and every fifty years property would go back to the families to whom it had originally been assigned.

Now move on to the New Testament. Listen, as a poor person, a near slave, to these words about God sung by Mary when she heard that Jesus was to be born:

"[God] has scattered the proud in the imagination of their hearts,
he has put down the mighty from their thrones,
and exalted those of low degree;
he has filled the hungry with good things,
and the rich he has sent empty away." (Luke 1:51–53)

Talk about good news! It is said that medieval peasants used to cheer when that passage was read each Christmas Eve. Listen to just one more text as though you were literally poor. Jesus says:

"Blessed are you poor, for yours is the kingdom of God.
"Blessed you that hunger now, for you shall be satisfied. . . .
"But woe to you that are rich. . . .
"Woe to you that are full now, for you shall hunger."
(Luke 6:20–21, 24–25)

Don't try somehow to "spiritualize" these verses. Take them as they stand, and you have good news for the poor.

Not only the Bible but also history must be read from the perspective of the poor. History has usually been written, Gutiérrez says, "with a white hand," that is to say, from the perspective of the oppressors. While history sounds one way when written from the point of view of the Spanish conquerors, which is our usual way of presenting it, it is quite different when written from the perspective of the Indians who were conquered. In the United States we have seen how different our history appears when Alex Haley writes *Roots* from the perspective of his slave ancestors. Liberation theologians must look at the history of church and state in that same way.

For the liberation theologian deeds must have priority over words. At the end of his most famous work, *A Theology of Liberation,* Gutiérrez writes that "all the political theologies, the theologies of hope, of revolution, and of liberation, are not worth one act of genuine solidarity with exploited social classes.'" No, *action* in solidarity with the poor must come first. The task of theology is to reflect in the light of the gospel upon one's experience in sharing with the struggles of the poor. Priority must be given to what Gutiérrez and his followers always like to call *praxis.* It means deeds, acts, action, as well as reflection on those acts. If it sometimes seems a bit foolish that the Greek term is always used, it may help us to understand if we remember that the fifth book of the New Testament is entitled "The *Praxis* of the Apostles." Remember our *Time* reporter who found liberation theology "curious"? Here was one curious feature: "No ivory-tower thinkers, the Latin American liberation theologians developed their ideas while working among those poor."[8] Liberation theology must be theology done by the poor and those who are actively identifying with the poor in their particular struggle.

This requirement gives a certain modesty to their claims. When a reporter from *The Christian Century* asked Gutiérrez to comment on the situation in Israel, he simply refused. "I am not the head of a religious world movement that is concerned about every problem in the world. I have an opinion, a small one, as an ordinary citizen."[9] He is sympathetic, or course, with the struggles of Blacks in the United States, of peoples in Asia, and of women around the world, but, since he is not personally involved in their struggle, he does not attempt to pontificate about what they should do. Each oppressed group must work out its own theology of liberation as it reflects on its own experiences. What all liberation theologians do have in common is this: they attempt to do theology, as Gutiérrez puts it, "from the *underside.*"

If you are thinking that this bias in behalf of the oppressed—this "Marxist" concern to overturn society in behalf of those on the bottom—sounds *subversive,* you are beginning to understand very well. "Subversion" is precisely the word Gutiérrez likes to use. He thinks it is Christian, not just communist. Christianity has always been for the *version* part of that word, *con*version, change, repentance. Yet we have settled too long for *super*version, change by and for the people on top. True repentance would be *sub*version, revolution achieved by and for those masses on the bottom.

I find myself tempted to protest, "Look, this is a biased theology. Granted that there is something good about it being biased in behalf of the poor, isn't it still a theological effort to bless the selfish concerns of the lower class and thus still a biased theology?"

Gutiérrez, however, has a powerful reply. The Bible from start to finish tells us that God, too, is biased—biased in behalf of the poor. The biblical prophets, the Mosaic law, and the Son of God have all told us that God is the defender of the orphan, the old person, the sick, and the destitute. The Jerusalem Bible's translation of Psalm 103:6 says it all: "Yahweh, who does what is right, is always on the side of the oppressed." The theologian who would be on God's side knows, therefore, which side to choose.

Marxism and Liberation

One fact about Gutiérrez' liberation theology strikes most North Americans as not simply "curious" but shocking: Gutiérrez is admittedly influenced by Marxist analysis of the economic situation. He is sure that the liberation needed by the poor of Latin America includes liberation from exploitation by the United States and by capitalism. Certainly it is difficult for me personally to understand this, but if we are to understand Gutiérrez we must try.

First, Gutiérrez affirms, it need not shock us that a theologian uses an economic analysis borrowed from an admittedly atheist philosopher. *Theology* means "talking (or thinking) about God." All of us, when we talk or think about God or about any other subject, think in the pattern of some philosophy. Augustine certainly thought about God and the gospel using the thought forms of the pagan Neoplatonists. Thomas Aquinas thought about God using the categories of the pagan Aristotle. Nineteenth-century theology thought about God using insights from the not-very-orthodox Christian Hegel. In itself there is nothing wrong with one's using the economic analysis of Karl Marx. After all, Marx' goal was "from each according to his ability; to each according to his need." That really is not so very different from Jesus' "Golden Rule."

For most of us a more serious problem is that Marxists think of the world as inevitably involved in a struggle between two economic classes. It is the rich fighting against the poor. Marx felt that this struggle must invariably be violent. Can a Christian become involved in this violent class conflict? Gutiérrez' reply is that violent class struggle is simply a fact of life in Latin America. Armed by our United States tax dollars, military dictatorships in Brazil, Colombia, Chile have imprisoned, tortured, and killed those who

European theology, he notes, has been preoccupied for many years with defending the faith against those skeptics who question the truth of Christianity, even the validity of belief in God. Bonhoeffer, for example, asked how we can speak of God in "a world come of age," but Latin American theology must speak to a very different problem. Its people are at least nominally Roman Catholic; they are not questioning whether God exists. The masses in Latin America are not in danger of becoming *nonbelievers* but *nonpersons.* That is, extreme poverty is stripping them of their dignity as human beings. Liberation theology must speak to that concern.

Traditional Doctrines and Liberation Theology

We have been looking at the basis and the method of liberation theology. Now we are ready to look at its actual doctrinal content. As already noted, Gutiérrez really is a rather orthodox Christian. True, he urges that ortho-praxis (right action) is more important than ortho-doxy (right beliefs), but the Vatican commission was not able to find any heresies through which to discredit this "disturber of the peace." Nevertheless Gutiérrez does have a particular emphasis even when discussing very traditional doctrines. (Incidentally, I have not read any discussion by him of doctrines disputed by Protestants, such as the infallibility of the Pope. Mary as the singer of the Magnificat is important to him, but traditional controversies about her "immaculate conception" or her assumption into heaven do not seem to be of special importance to this particular Roman Catholic.)

Here are some doctrines he does discuss.

The *Bible* he calls "the word of God." We have already noted that what is unique about Gutiérrez' approach to Scripture is his concern that we read it from the particular perspective of the poor.

Sin to Gutiérrez is selfishness, and it is not only individual but also social. Robert McAfee Brown wrote me that while teaching in New York in 1977 Gutiérrez became an avid reader of Walter Rauschenbusch. Those who know Rauschenbusch's social gospel will find that words like the following sound familiar:

have protested in behalf of the poor. We finance the war in l Salvador and support terrorists against Nicaragua. Gutiérrez di not invent the violent class struggle; it is simply a fact of Lati American life. The question is merely on which side ought th church to be, and how should we be related to it.

It is important to note, though, that however much we in the United States may support violence with our tax dollars Gutiérrez is not a great advocate of violence. He tried to dissuade Camilo Torres from joining the guerrillas. I have not read any passage in Gutiérrez in which he advocates violence. Rather he protests the violence of those who ruthlessly put down all efforts of those who would change the economic system. The poor, he says, are victims also of what he calls "institutional violence." People who are forced to live at near starvation levels, subject to every disease, in ignorance and fear of military police, are already the victims of violence even if *physical* violence is not used against them. To such "institutional violence" he is unalterably opposed.

Moreover Gutiérrez is critical of what he calls "the Theology of Revolution." No military might, he knows, is going to bring in the kingdom of God. His personal involvement in the struggle is with a community center in Lima, with education, and with the grass-roots fellowships of which we took note earlier. He is no preacher of terrorism.

I cannot find any place in which Gutiérrez expresses any praise for Soviet Russia. He says that the church in Cuba is called to a twofold task, to support what is humanizing and to criticize what is dehumanizing in its revolution. He attacks what he calls "baptizing the revolution." He writes:

> The gospel message is a message that can never be identified with any concrete social formula, however just that formula may seem to us at the moment. The word of the Lord is a challenge to its every historical incarnation and places that incarnation in the broad perspective of the radical and total liberation of Christ, the Lord of history.[10]

He is probably more willing to criticize the socialism he advocates than most of us are to criticize the capitalism we take for granted.

In part Gutiérrez explains his interest in Marxism in this way.

To sin is to refuse to love one's neighbors and, therefore, the Lord himself. Sin—a breach of friendship with God and others—is according to the Bible the ultimate cause of poverty, injustice, and the oppression in which men live. In describing sin as the ultimate cause we do not in any way negate the structural reasons and the objective determinants leading to these situations. It does, however, emphasize the fact that things do not happen by chance and that behind an unjust structure :here is a personal or collective will responsible—a willingness to reject God and neighbor.[11]

There are sinful structures, economic systems, and political patterns. Sinful as these are, however, they rest upon selfishness in the human heart.

Salvation is liberation. This, of course, is a central concept in Gutiérrez' thought. He analyzes liberation (salvation) as having a threefold meaning.

In the first place, *liberation* expresses the aspirations of oppressed peoples and social classes, emphasizing the conflictual aspect of the economic, social, and political process which puts them at odds with wealthy nations and oppressive classes. . . . At a deeper level, *liberation* can be applied to an understanding of history. Man is seen as assuming conscious responsibility for his own destiny. . . . In this perspective the unfolding of all of man's dimensions is demanded. . . . The gradual conquest of true freedom leads to the creation of a new man and a qualitatively different society. . . .

Finally . . . Christ the Savior liberates man from sin, which is the ultimate root of all disruption of friendship and of all injustice and oppression. Christ makes man truly free, that is to say, he enables man to live in communion with him; and this is the basis for all human brotherhood.[12]

These are not three separate processes, of course, but are simply three different aspects of the salvation Christ brings. Salvation thus involves also a new relationship with one's fellow human beings.

But St. Paul asserts not only that Christ liberated us; he also tells us that he did it in order that we might be free. Free for what? Freed to love. . . . The fullness of liberation—a free gift from Christ—is communion with God and with other men.[13]

Jesus Christ is, therefore, the Liberator.

> In Christ the all-comprehensiveness of the liberating process reaches its fullest sense. His work encompasses the three levels of meaning which we mentioned above. . . . "All the dynamism of the cosmos and of human history, the movement towards the creation of a more just and fraternal world, the overcoming of social inequalities among men, the efforts . . . to liberate man from all that depersonalizes him—physical and moral misery, ignorance, and hunger . . . all these originate, are transformed, and reach their perfection in the saving work of Christ. In him and through him salvation is present at the heart of man's history."[14]

In him the Word is *made* human; we are not just given a word *about* human beings. God *became* human in Christ.

Evangelism is the proclamation of the good news of the liberation Christ came to bring us. Gutiérrez appears not to be greatly concerned to try to persuade everyone to become a Roman Catholic, but he is interested in evangelism, in telling the good news.

> To know that the Lord loves us, to accept the free gift of his love, is the deep source of the joy and gladness of a person who lives by the word of God. Evangelization is the communication of this joy. It is the communication of the good news of the love of God that has changed our life.[15]

Evangelism must be carried out by the poor themselves if it is to be genuinely liberating. To the rich, that may mean that it will "not sound nice and it will not smell good," but it will bring genuine conversion.

Conversion involves a change both of the individual *and of society,* as Rauschenbusch well knew. It is conversion "*to* the neighbor." "To be converted is to commit oneself to the process of the liberation of the poor and oppressed, to commit oneself lucidly, realistically, and concretely."[16] One might protest against his concern for changes in the structures of society. He pictures a critic demanding, "What is the good of changing the structures without a change in the human heart?" Gutiérrez replies:

> This is only a half truth, for changing social and cultural structures is a way of changing the human heart. There is a mutual dependency, and reciprocal demands, between the human heart and its social milieu, based on a radical unity. It is no more "mechanistic" to think that a

structural change automatically makes for a new humanity, than to think that a "personal" change guarantees social transformations. Both assumptions are unreal and naive.[17]

Gutiérrez, like Rauschenbusch before him, is concerned for evangelism and conversion which are not simply quantitative, reaching more and more people, but which are qualitative, effecting deeper and deeper changes in the hearts of individuals and in the institutions of society.

Spirituality is not neglected but enhanced, Gutiérrez feels, by his approach. At this writing Gutiérrez is under attack from the Vatican and from the Peruvian hierarchy. They charge that because he uses Marx and talks of economics and politics he is a "materialist." On the contrary, he likes to cite Matthew 25:31–46 as implying that Christians meet Christ as they become involved with "the least of these," Christ's brothers and sisters. "To be followers of Jesus requires that they walk with and be committed to the poor; when they do, they experience an encounter with the Lord who is simultaneously revealed and hidden in the faces of the poor (see Matt. 25:31–46)."[18] Earlier he had written:

> The poor person, the other, becomes the revealer of the Utterly Other. . . . Conversion is an absolute abandonment of oneself and an opening up to God and others. . . . Encounter with Christ in the poor person constitutes an authentic spiritual experience. It is life in the Spirit.[19]

One whole section of *A Theology of Liberation* is devoted to "A Spirituality of Liberation" (pp. 203–208). The Eucharist, the Lord's Supper, Gutiérrez reminds us, involves our fellowship with others as together we feed upon Christ. In fact, the whole of Gutiérrez' latest book is devoted to the spiritual dimension. He simply wants to emphasize with 1 John 4:7 that we must actively "love one another; for love is of God, and he who loves is born of God and knows God." That book, *We Drink from Our Own Wells,* ends:

> Spirituality is a community enterprise. It is the passage of a people through the solitude and dangers of the desert, as it carves out its own way in the following of Jesus Christ. This spiritual experience is the well from which we must drink. From it we draw the promise of resurrection.[20]

Finally, among his doctrines to be discussed here *eschatology* is of high importance to Gutiérrez. We have seen that prophets are not simply social reformers. They are women and men with a vision of the future. Like the others we have considered, Gutiérrez is no naïve optimist. It is, however, his faith that some day "the people will snatch the gospel out of the hands of their dominators, never more to permit it to be utilized for the justification of a situation contrary to the will of the God who liberates."[21] Did he come to this hope simply through romantic illusion? "No, rather a clear awareness that something new was afoot, something no repression could ever again quell or crush: a people's will to self-affirmation and to life."[22]

The opening sentences of *We Drink from Our Own Wells* help summarize much of Gutiérrez' theology of liberation.

> A Christian is identified as a follower of Jesus, and reflection on the experience of following constitutes the central theme of any solid theology. The experience and the reflection alike have for their subject a community that under the movement of the Spirit focuses its life on the proclamation of the good news: the Lord is risen! Death and injustice are not the final word of history. Christianity is a message of life, a message based on the gratuitous love of the Father for us.[23]

Concluding Comments

What is a white, Anglo-Saxon North American Protestant to say about the thought of this foreign Roman Catholic? "Curious"? Certainly! "Radical" and "subversive"? Deliberately! "Heretical"? No! Some four hundred biblical citations in *A Theology of Liberation* and a proportionate number in *We Drink From Our Own Wells* help to underline the disturbing fact that Gutiérrez is another prophet of biblical truth. There are some cautions which Gutiérrez himself would be the first to suggest. One is that he is speaking to the situation in Latin America. He modestly refuses to try to say what should be done in other lands and cultures.

Prophets involved in other struggles by the oppressed have been influenced by his message but have applied it in different ways. James Cone has written *A Black Theology of Liberation.*[24] "God is black," Cone tells us, and in the light of Gutiérrez' work we can better understand this Black thinker's affirmation that in Christ God has identified with Cone's fellow victims of racial oppression. Rosemary Radford Ruether and other women have made use of similar ideas in their prophetic call for women's liberation, but what does Gutiérrez say to the white, male Protestant in the United States?

It is interesting that each of our prophets has been a kind of socialist. Yet an uncritical adoption of socialism here may not be any more required than our violent defense of capitalism in Latin America. Critics of Marx deny that history can be explained simply around the struggle of economic classes. There are, they argue, values which capitalism preserves which are important to human dignity and development, even as there are those values which socialism seeks to protect. Individual initiative and enterprise may enhance freedom and help reduce poverty, and some economists propose that the capitalistic system has helped to give the United States "the richest poor in the world." Gutiérrez affirms but perhaps does not need to stress for North American readers the dangers which one may observe in socialism of the Russian or Chinese style. Democracy need not require capitalism, but communism and democracy have not yet been successfully blended. Perhaps a case can be made for some kind of rough mixture of socialism and capitalism as the best likely option at least for our own country.[25] Nevertheless Gutiérrez helps remind us that we cannot be content with American capitalism as long as fifteen percent of our people are officially poor! The recent letter of the North American Roman Catholic bishops dealing with economic injustices here reminds us how far short of the ideal our system actually falls.

At the moment of this writing the United States government is running budget deficits of catastrophic proportions. These, we are told, are necessary to provide the arms and hire the soldiers which can crush the steady spread of Russian communism from Cuba and Nicaragua to all of Latin America. The "evil empire," we are told, is spreading. Gutiérrez reminds us that the socialist movement in Latin America is not the product of Russian propaganda or influence. It is based on the determination of the poor no longer to watch their babies die. We need to understand this. We need radically to revise our policy toward Latin America.

A student of the Bible from a North American background may want to question more than does Gutiérrez whether the gospel is really a call to the disadvantaged to unite and throw off their chains. Gutiérrez himself affirms that Jesus was no socialist agitator. The prophets spoke to the rich and the rulers as well as to the poor and oppressed. There is, however, no comfort in that for us, for what they said was a warning of judgment upon the rich if they did not change their ways!

A Protestant may want to place more emphasis on the element of forgiveness in salvation than does Gutiérrez. My *praxis* will never be good enough to win God's favor. Salvation means forgiveness, reconciliation, received as a gift by faith. Once again, however, the emphasis on forgiveness, reconciliation, and love may point us all the more to the need for loving concern for the victims of our sin.

Gutiérrez, however, is not just interested in liberation for one class. We who are affluent need liberation, too. Perhaps his thought can help to set us free from the chains of tradition, fear, prejudice, and greed. Then we, too, may find our place in that coming kingdom of God.

Study Suggestions

1. One text is so identified with liberation theology that the best way to begin study of the thought of Gutiérrez or any other liberation theologian is to review it. Though Luke evidently knows that Jesus' sermon in Nazareth was not his first, Luke carefully puts it first in his account of Jesus' message. Matthew begins with the Sermon on the Mount and Mark with the story of the casting out of a demon, and they both summarize Jesus' message as the proclamation of the kingdom of God. Luke, however, begins with Jesus' announcement of liberation. Begin this study, therefore, by looking again at Luke 4:18 and Jesus'

proclamation of freedom to the captives and good news to the poor.

2. Chapter 3 begins with a rather gloomy picture of the condition of the Latin American poor and suggests that there are many of our southern neighbors who blame their troubles in part on North American capitalism. It is difficult for us, who have prospered in this system and who love our country, to hear this criticism with much sympathy. It might be good if you or your study group could review briefly some of the less happy aspects of our history in relation to Latin America. Perhaps a high school history teacher could visit your group and try to present some of these as seen through Latin eyes. Of course, we see ourselves justly as having done much good to our neighbors in the south, but try to imagine how some of them must feel as they recall such historic events as the following. We invaded Mexico and took from them most of what is now the western United States. The Spanish American War made Cuba heavily dependent upon us. We seized the area for the Panama Canal. When the repressive Batista dictatorship we had supported failed, we attempted an invasion of Cuba at the Bay of Pigs. ITT and the CIA cooperated to overthrow the democratically elected government of Chile in the early 1970s. We sent our armed forces into Granada in the 1980s. We have repeatedly provided the arms and money which have kept in power the worst dictatorships in that region, often citing our fear of socialism as the reason. Also, from whatever high motives, we are at this writing supporting the Contras in their raids on villages in Nicaragua. This review is not meant to propose that the United States has failed to do much good but simply to help the reader understand how some in Latin America may distrust us and our capitalistic system.

3. The basis of liberation theology is Bible study done from the perspective of the poor. Therefore study Isaiah 61:1; Psalm 68:5; Jeremiah 22:13, 15–16 and ask yourself and others, if you are studying with a group, how you would understand these verses if you were poverty stricken. List the ideas that would come to you as in your poverty you heard these words.

4. Pp. 60–62 describe the Marxism which has caused the Vatican

concern (even publicly televised!) about liberation theology. You might make a list of those things about socialism which seem anti-Christian and those, if any, which could be understood as reflecting the economics of Acts 2:44–45 and 4:32. Does Gutiérrez seem to be advocating the bad aspects of socialism or those which might be good? How do you and others react to the socialist principle "from each according to his ability; to each according to his need"?

5. Pp. 52–66 briefly summarize Gutiérrez' theology doctrine by doctrine. How does it compare with that of Rauschenbusch? How does it compare with the Apostles' Creed and other traditional statements of theology?

6. One criticism which has been made of liberation theology is that it stresses economics but neglects personal devotion. If possible look at a copy of Gutiérrez' *We Drink from Our Own Wells* to see his emphasis on prayer. At least review p. 65 with this question in mind. How directly is prayer related to economics in your own theology? Do you pray before making a business decision or before accepting a salary increase?

7. The last pages of the chapter offer some criticisms of liberation theology. Do you and others regard them as valid, too few, or not strong enough? If you are in a group, take a vote and give your reasons for your choice.

8. What groups other than Latin American peasants need liberation today? List them. What is your church doing to help those who are working for their freedom?

9. Gutiérrez himself would far rather we be actually *doing* something to aid the oppressed in their struggle than that we study his writings. What might you and others actually *do* in response to reading this chapter?

4

Rosemary Radford Ruether and Feminist Theology

"You know that the rulers of the Gentiles lord it over them, and their great men exercise authority over them. It shall not be so among you." (Matthew 20:25–26)

At least according to the blurb on the paperback edition, it was not the Bible that was "the famous best seller that ignited women's liberation." It was Betty Friedan's *The Feminine Mystique*.

Friedan had done research among her fellow alumnae of Smith College. She found these highly educated and capable women suffering from a kind of unnamed malaise. She wrote of it:

THE PROBLEM LAY BURIED, UNSPOKEN, FOR MANY years in the minds of American women. It was a strange stirring, a sense of dissatisfaction, a yearning that women suffered in the middle of the twentieth century in the United States. Each suburban wife struggled with it alone. As she made the beds, shopped for groceries, matched slipcover material, ate peanut butter sandwiches with her children, chauffeured Cub Scouts and Brownies, lay beside her husband at night—she was afraid to ask even of herself the silent question—"Is this all?"[1]

Friedan found that women were repeatedly told

how to breastfeed children and handle their toilet training, how to cope with sibling rivalry and adolescent rebellion; how to buy a dishwasher, bake bread, cook gourmet snails, and build a swimming pool with their own hands; how to dress, look, and act more feminine and make marriage more exciting; how to keep their husbands from dying young and their sons from growing into delinquents. They were taught to pity the neurotic, unfeminine, unhappy women who wanted to be poets or physicists or presidents.[2]

Nowhere were women being encouraged to be all they were capable of becoming, of realizing their potential as free, intelligent, whole persons. Friedan was sure, however, that things were about to change. "The time is at hand when the voices of the feminine mystique can no longer drown out the inner voice that is driving women on to become complete."[3] She was right! In 1963 the time had come. In the revolutionary sixties women's liberation was to grow into a powerful, disturbing movement.

Betty Friedan was not a theologian. *The Feminine Mystique* discussed religion for only two of its three hundred and eighty-four pages and then only to denounce the "traditional resistance of religious orthodoxy." Half of one of those pages was a quotation from a manual designed to help Roman Catholic (male celibate) priests discourage married women from taking work outside the home. Presbyterians, Friedan noted, do ordain women, but in 1963 less than one percent of their pastors were females. It was Mary Daly who five years after Friedan's book worked out the implications of Friedan's brief attack on religion: she renounced the Christianity of her Roman Catholic tradition. The very title of Daly's book called for her readers to advance *Beyond God the Father*. She conceded the possibility that "Jesus was a feminist, but so what? . . . Even if he wasn't, *I am*."[4] No male figure from the past could serve as a model for women in the twentieth century. "A patriarchal divinity or his son is exactly *not* in a position to save us from the horrors of a patriarchal world."[5]

Daly's challenge was not to go unanswered. Thousands of women, sometimes supported in their concern by thousands of men, who now include newly ordained women clergy, have demonstrated that the church can be in the forefront of the struggle for justice and freedom for women. One of the many who have undertaken this task is the subject of this chapter. She has been perhaps the most prolific and forceful writer of all the feminist theologians. We turn now to the thought of Rosemary Radford Ruether.

Life

Ruether wrote in *Commonweal:*

> I grew up in a relatively privileged, patriotic, and pious family. Other than my immediate family, most of my relatives on both sides are politically conservative and "genteelly" chauvinist and racist. Why I have instinctively moved in a different direction through various experiences of social contradiction is something I can't explain. Perhaps it should be called "grace." . . . For me, a recognition of the abhorrent behavior of the Roman Catholic church preceded an awareness of the contradictions of American society. I got this, oddly enough, by reading history. I remember one of my first "shock" experiences when I was about eighteen in thé medieval history class. The professor mentioned casually that the church did not oppose slavery or serfdom.[6]

Repelled by such lack of concern for justice on the part of the church and attracted by the thought of professors who had rejected Christianity for other meaningful understandings of life, she tended to move away from her Catholic upbringing for a little while. Nevertheless she soon came to realize that for her the Christian faith was what offered the best way to express the nature of human existence and our relationship to God. It was an ecumenical Christianity she adopted. She has worshiped in churches of many denominations, spoken at schools of many denominations, and now teaches at Garrett-Evangelical Theological Seminary, a Methodist institution. Yet she remains a Roman Catholic.

One is amazed at her activities. At present still in her forties, she is the author or editor of seventeen books, has contributed to thirty-six others, and has written more than four hundred and fifty articles and reviews! Someone computed that between 1965 and 1976 she had filled approximately one hundred and twenty-five different speaking engagements on university campuses or at church conventions! Yet she is also a wife and the mother of three children. (That combination of motherhood and a busy career outside the home suggests that she and her husband must have achieved something of the partnership in marriage which she pictures as the ideal.)

We are here going to deal especially with Ruether as a Christian involved in the struggle for women's liberation. That cause, however, has been by no means her only interest. Her writings repeatedly express concern about ecology. One whole book of hers is an attack on anti-Semitism. Another volume, entitled *Liberation Theology: Human Hope Confronts Christian History and American Power*, was published one year before Gutiérrez' work was translated into English: in it she had already paid tribute to Gutiérrez as "perhaps the leading theologian of Latin America." Also, while still in her twenties she spent a summer working for civil rights in Mississippi. Of those difficult days she writes:

> Here, for the first time, I learned to look at America from the Black side; to see safety in the Black community and danger in nightriding whites or white officers of the law. In subsequent experiences, both in the American ghettos of race and poverty and in Latin America, I have deepened that experience.[7]

She calls Martin Luther King, Jr. "the most skilled exponent in recent American history (perhaps all of American history) of American civil religion in prophetic criticism and liberation." Ruether in fact devoted ten years of her life to teaching at Howard School of Religion, a divinity school at a predominantly Black university. She was very involved in the peace movement in the sixties and she writes of participating in numerous "sing-ins," "pray-ins," and "die-ins." She even spent nights in jails after being arrested in peace demonstrations.

One thing which binds together all these ethical concerns and also her loving criticisms of her church's hierarchical system is this:

as a Christian she opposes the domination, which sometimes becomes almost enslavement, of any people by others. The centuries-old repression of women is one example of such domination. It is to her protest as a feminist theologian against sexism throughout history that we now turn.

Sexism in History

"We are a people with a history," Ruether writes to her fellow Christians, "much of it bad. But its bad parts also teach lessons that we should not forget." It was in a history class that she was shocked into a new awareness that the church needed to be more involved in the struggle for justice. Historical theology became her major field of study, and over and over her books review the sad history of the repression of women.

Sexism is, of course, much older than Christianity. In fact, says Ruether, it is the oldest form of human oppression. Some radical feminists have actually proposed a kind of revival of ancient pagan religions which included goddesses along with gods. Ruether points out that historically these religions did not keep women from being a repressed group. Typically, while a goddess might be revered as the source of life, that life was for her *son* who ruled.

It is the all too often sexist history of the church that Ruether most often reviews. Here is one of her favorite examples of the attitude toward women which came too nearly to dominate medieval Christendom. It is Tertullian's address to women as daughters of Eve.

> *You* are the Devil's gateway. *You* are the unsealer of that forbidden tree. *You* are the first deserter of the divine law. *You* are she who persuaded him whom the Devil was not valiant enough to attack. *You* destroyed so easily God's image man. On account of *your* desert, that is death, even the Son of God had to die.[8]

Among thinkers like Tertullian women were not simply thought inferior; they were condemned as the very source of evil. True, they were often considered as but little more intelligent than animals. Thomas Aquinas, following Aristotle, who grouped women with slaves, taught that women were "misbegotten males." The corruption of women, however, was regarded as much more sinister than mere stupidity. Ruether notes that the words "matter" and "mother" are obviously close kin. The medieval ideal was the "spiritual" life. Such a life, it seemed, must be lived in separation from evil matter, and hence from those whose role is to be mothers. Women came to represent the body, the carnal, and hence what was regarded as evil. Among others Ruether quotes Augustine: "I find nothing so casts down the manly mind from its heights as the fondling of women and those bodily contacts which belong to the married state." Women were believed to be "naturally" prone to witchcraft.

The age of chivalry and later the romantic era brought, Ruether says, a curious reversal of this dualism. Then it was the woman who became the symbol of spirit. The *macho* male was supposed to be involved in the "real world." The "lady" was idealized as the incarnation of morality and all the values for which brutish men could find no time in the jungle of business and war. Women were supposed to be above sexual desire as above all evil, that being the male sphere. Even in marriage they were to be the passive objects of their husbands' pleasure. They were not to be involved in business, politics, or anything else worldly. They were, Ruether says, to be "half angel, half idiot." Woman was "the tranquilized tranquilizer," the goddess of the home. This isolation, of course, was only the ideal. Actually, with the industrial revolution the women of the poor were often forced into wage slavery at far less pay than that received by men for the same sweatshop labor.

In spite of all this, history did produce heroines. Ruether writes, for example, of those ascetic "Mothers of the Church" who broke out of the set roles prescribed for women and founded early convents. They were in a sense pioneers of women's liberation. There were those noble Roman women who became followers of the great Jerome. That biblical translator was persuaded by Marcella to teach her Hebrew. Sometimes she kept him up half the night dictating answers to her questions. Another of his female companions, Paula, became even better at Hebrew than Jerome and established a community of some fifty virgins who provided a hospice for travelers. Yet another of this group, Melania, visited the great fourth-century hermits of Egypt. To travel at night she sometimes had to disguise herself as a slave. Arrested, she was released when she revealed that she was a nobleman's widow. She founded a monastery at the Mount of Olives. There women devoted themselves to charitable work, copying manuscripts, Bible study, and prayer. Though the church did offer women such vocations, it required of them that they renounce their identity as sexual beings in order to accept such work, and even the most dedicated virgin still could not hope to attain a place in the power structure of the church, its clergy.

Ruether likes to tell of brave nonconformists like Mary Dyer. When she supported Anne Hutchenson in the 1640s, she was expelled from the Massachusetts Colony and forced to flee to Rhode Island. In 1660, though, she returned to Massachusetts as a Quaker missionary, was arrested, compelled to watch her companions as they were hung, and then was blindfolded and led to the gallows. Reprieved, she returned to preach again. This time she was martyred by the orthodox Puritans.

As a Roman Catholic Ruether is especially interested in the place in history of one enormously important woman, the Virgin Mary. She traces that history with complete candor. The roots of some aspects of the medieval cult of the Virgin she traces back to pagan origins. The Greeks revered both virgin goddesses and goddesses of sexuality and maternity as "inferior powers." In Egypt Isis was worshiped as the queen of heaven and redeeming wisdom. The New Testament does not, according to Ruether, present Mary as perpetually virgin, nor is the virgin birth used to exalt virginity. The Gnostics, however, teaching a dualism of spirit vs. body and attempting to emphasize the one at the expense of the other, led in representing Mary as eternally "above" sex. In the Middle Ages Mary became the personification of two ideals. She was the virgin, "unsoiled" by sexual intercourse, and she was the model mother, the submissive female. Eventually Mary came almost to replace Christ as savior and mediator.

The paradox of the just and merciful God is dissolved into divine wrath (Jesus) and a human woman (Mary) representing mercy. She, like an understanding mother, can make allowances for the inadequacies of human nature. As Christ becomes more to be feared, trust is transferred to Mary. Devotion to her can guarantee that even the worst sinner has a chance of salvation. A mother's heart is much too tender to allow even the most wayward child to be cast off irreconcilably. (Fathers apparently are not so forgiving!)[9]

Stories of a miraculous birth of Mary and of her assumption into heaven became church dogma. If Christ continued as the way to salvation, Mary became the way to Christ. She was worshiped, like Isis of Egypt, as the queen of heaven.

In the struggle for women's liberation, Ruether asks, which side is Mary on? Ruether's answer seems to be that it depends on how Mary is viewed. As the traditional symbol of the exaltation of celibacy, feminine submission, and the idealization of the medieval concept of the "lady," Mary is not helpful. There is, however, another way in which Mary may be regarded. Luke, Ruether notes, pictures Mary as actively cooperating with God in the incarnation, not stopping to ask Joseph's permission. It is Mary who sings the Magnificat with its glad announcement of the liberation in which God "has put down the mighty from their thrones, and exalted those of low degree" (Luke 1:52). She can be seen as the symbol of the oppressed to whom, the Gospel says, God comes. "Mary, or the church, represents liberated humanity. Mary represents the *person of the church* from the perspective of the conversion that has to go on in history and between people, to overcome dehumanizing power and suppressed personhood."[10] Mary can be viewed as an eschatological symbol, the oppressed at last freed to share in the creative work of God.

The Basis of Feminist Theology

The experience of women down through history is the starting point for Ruether's feminist theology. As Gutiérrez' liberation theology is reflection upon the struggle for freedom of the Latin American poor, as King's prophetic actions began in the ghetto of an Alabama city, and as Rauschenbusch's social gospel was evolved near Hell's Kitchen, so feminist theology, Ruether believes, must grow out of involvement with oppressed womankind. All theology, Ruether argues, is based on experience. Even the Bible itself is "codified human experience."

> The uniqueness of feminist theology lies not in its use of the criterion of experience but rather in its use of *women's* experience, which has been almost entirely shut out of theological reflection in the past. The use of women's experience in feminist theology, therefore, explodes as a critical force, exposing classical theology, including its codified traditions, as based on *male* experience rather than on universal human experience.[11]

There has always been "a sociology of theology," with a dominant group determining what should be considered "orthodox." Feminist theology will have its own standard of judgment:

> The critical principle of feminist theology is the promotion of the full humanity of women. Whatever denies, diminishes, or distorts the full humanity of women is, therefore, appraised as not redemptive . . . what does promote the full humanity of women is of the Holy.[12]

Ruether is aware of the truth in Mary Daly's charge that there is sexism in the Bible. Paul or, more often, Ruether believes, later disciples writing in Paul's name could command that women must keep silent in the churches and could speak of hierarchical relationships, Christ over man over woman. God is spoken of in language which implies that God is male. Repeatedly women are told to be subject to their husbands (Eph. 5:22; Col. 3:18; 1 Peter 3:1). Women are even told that their salvation lies in their bearing children (1 Tim. 2:15). The Bible was written in and does often reflect a sexist culture. Similarly, there are biblical passages which also condone slavery. As late as the 1860s these were used to defend slavery as part of God's "patriarchal government." However, just as we now realize that the passages condoning slavery reflect the limitations of their setting, so we must recognize that the sexist passages are reflections of the culture in which they were written. The central message of the Bible is the prophetic call for justice and freedom.

Thus, as with our other modern prophets, it is to the biblical prophets that Ruether repeatedly turns. The prophetic-liberating tradition is "the central tradition, the tradition by which Biblical faith constantly criticizes and renews itself and its own vision."[13] The prophets spoke out for the oppressed. Feminist theology simply calls attention to another group of the oppressed, extending the call for justice to include the needs of women.

Indeed, with Jesus one finds incarnate the concern to treat people of both sexes equally as persons. Jesus chose women to be among his friends and disciples. They traveled with him and were more faithful at his death than was Peter. He could hold up a poor widow as an example (Luke 21:1-4) and talk freely with one who was both a Samaritan and a woman (John 4). He healed women and even brought back from the dead the son of one widow (Luke 7:11-15). He commended Mary over Martha precisely at the moment when Mary had broken out of the traditional role for women (Luke 10:41-42). It is no wonder that consistent tradition makes a woman, Mary Magdalene, a first witness to the resurrection and a messenger of it to the male apostles. Jesus applied the teachings of the Sermon on the Mount to all persons, regardless of sex.

Whatever Paul or later authors writing in his name may have said in particular situations, Paul is pictured also as regarding Priscilla as a partner, as well as Euodia and Synteche, recognizing Phoebe as a deaconess, accepting the hospitality and friendship of Lydia, and even proposing that a wife should rule over her husband's body (1 Cor. 7:4). Whatever he may have written at other times, Paul knew that "there is neither male nor female; for you are all one in Christ Jesus" (Gal. 3:28). Yet the passages which best summarize Ruether's emphasis are especially those which describe the essence of Christianity in terms of the rejection of domination by anyone over anyone else. She likes to quote these words of Jesus:

> You know that the rulers of the Gentiles lord it over them, and their great men exercise authority over them. It shall not be so among you; but whoever would be great among you must be your servant, and whoever would be first among you must be your slave; even as the Son

but Ruether recognizes Jesus as the champion of all the downtrodden on earth.

> Jesus seems to express a radicalized view of the concept of a coming Reign of God as a time of the vindication of the poor and oppressed. The poor and the oppressed are not seen in nationalist terms as Israel, but rather as marginalized groups and classes within the Jewish world of his day. . . . Jesus' vision of the Kingdom is neither nationalistic nor other-worldly. The coming Reign of God is expected to happen on earth, as the Lord's Prayer makes evident (God's Kingdom come, God's will be done on earth).[14]

(Walter Rauschenbusch would have liked that statement!) Today we recognize that women are among those who are oppressed. The good news is Christ's promise that those who have been last, including women, may yet be first in the coming kingdom of God.

The cross is also described in words not unlike those of Rauschenbusch.

> I became aware that the root idea of Christ is not that of personal and other-worldly salvation, but of social and historical salvation from the massive contradiction of collective human apostasy. This is the meaning of Jesus's crucifixion; not a deterministic "self-sacrifice" for individual "sins," but a political assassination on the cross of collective apostasy by the political and religious institutions that claim authority over our lives.[15]

Sin is understood as both personal and social, but feminist theology has its special emphasis.

> Feminism presumes a radical concept of "sin." It claims that a most basic expression of human community, the I-Thou relation as the relationship of men and women, has been distorted throughout all known history into an oppressive relationship that has victimized one-half of the human race and turned the other half into tyrants.[16]

There is a danger in the frequently expressed view that sin is pride. What many women need is to be delivered from self-abnegation to a proper measure of self-esteem.

Conversion, therefore, will bring women a new sense of the right kind of pride and with it the reestablishment of right relationships between people. It may be necessary for women to become angry, to move through a sense of the bitterness of of man came not to be served but to serve, and to give his life as ransom for many. (Matt. 20:25-28)

Among Christians, she is sure, domination by males or by any other group should have no place.

Feminist theology, then, seeks its foundation in the experience of women, past and present, and in the prophetic call for justice and equality which echoes throughout the Scripture. To the tenets of that theology we now turn.

Feminist Theology

To begin with, *God* in feminist theology is *not* male. Tradition has described the deity in such patriarchal language that it is difficult for us to think of the Divine One in other terms. True, the Bible does sometimes speak of a God who can "cry out like a woman in travail" (Isa. 42:14). Wisdom in Proverbs is spoken of as female. *Rechem,* the Hebrew word for compassion or mercy, is derived from the word for womb. Nevertheless the language of the Bible and of the church is usually so patriarchal and hierarchical that we find it difficult to remember that God is neither male nor female. Ruether has begun, therefore, to use the unpronounceable symbol "God/ess" as a reminder that the deity is not just a big dominant male.

Creation is the work of God and is good. It was God who created us with bodies, male and female, and saw that nature was "very good." Repeatedly Ruether cries out against the body-spirit dualism which devalues nature and associates women exclusively either with a flesh regarded as sinful or with an idealized, other-worldly "spiritual" perfection. Ecology and women's liberation both demand a new recognition that nature is God's good creation and that people are intended to be part of it.

Jesus was male, and feminism in the modern sense did not exist in his time. Must women then join Mary Daly in rejecting this male savior? Perhaps it might seem so to those who view him only as tradition presents him, with the church as his "bride" and with Christ represented there always by an exclusively male hierarchy, alienation, in order to rise to a new level of consciousness of a woman's humanity as a full person under God. Ruether warns, however, against a female chauvinism: the converted woman sees men as persons, too. The goal is not only liberation but also reconciliation.

Feminist *anthropology* (what other theologies have called "the doctrine of man") must dispense with old sexual stereotypes.

> There is no valid biological basis for labeling certain psychic capacities, such as reason, "masculine" and others, such as intuition, "feminine."
> . . . We need to affirm . . . that all humans possess a full and equivalent human nature and personhood, *as male and female*. . . . they need to appropriate and deepen the integration of the whole self . . . that is already theirs.[17]

Most especially, of course, the idea that some persons are inferior to others because of their sex must be abandoned. All are children of God.

Finally, among the doctrines of feminist theology to be reviewed here *the church* receives special attention. Ruether says that as a loyal Roman Catholic she feels it her responsibility to criticize Catholicism where it needs correcting, just as others should point out the flaws in their traditions. Thus she does not hesitate to question the dogma of papal infallibility, especially where papal pronouncements seem to reflect the sexism which she finds so characteristic of the church's historic attitude toward women. Following a 1977 papal statement on ordination she wrote:

> One might say that if the Vatican lost its credibility for "infallibility" in matters of morals with the birth-control controversy, it lost its credibility for "infallibility" in matters of faith with the declaration on the admission of women to the priesthood.[18]

A historian, she traces the sexism which has been characteristic of the church throughout nearly two thousand years. It is most clearly manifest in the church's exclusion of women from the ministry. A male god must be represented by male priests or ministers. Indeed, to Ruether the whole concept of a dominant priesthood or ministry over against a submissive laity must be questioned. Instead of a hierarchy the church needs servants who will teach the church to be a fellowship of ministry. She points to the Latin American *communidades de base* as examples of one kind of valid church activity. Ideally the church should be "the avant-garde of liberated humanity," a fellowship in which all domination of some by others has been overcome.

Ruether's Vision of the Future

We have seen that there is truth in the popular picture of the prophet as one who looks to the future. Rauschenbusch had faith that the kingdom would come. King had a dream. Gutiérrez sees a great movement toward liberation. Ruether, too, writes with hope.

She is little interested, however, in traditional eschatology with its goal of the individual soul's escape from this world to a heaven after death. Indeed she regards this as having been of such questionable aid to the cause of liberation for women that she adopts an agnostic position toward the question of personal immortality. Instead she focuses on a kingdom which, as it comes, will mean God's will being done here on earth. For Ruether, as for our other "prophets," this means some kind of socialist economy.

> We must say then that the liberation of women as a caste is impossible within the present socio-economic system. Only in a system totally restructured in all its basic interdependencies . . . can women emerge into the full range of human activities now available to men. This probably means a revolutionary reform of society along the lines of communitarian socialism.[19]

However much other jobs and professions are opened to women, they cannot hope to achieve genuine equality of opportunity as long as the burden of housework and the responsibilities of child-rearing are not shared equally by men. The future must bring a new style of family life.

> The partnership marriage . . . means women as well as men contribute to the economic maintenance of the home. Men as well as women are equally parents and houseworkers. Most importantly, it means that men must be committed to their wives' full human development. . . . society will gain two skilled persons rather than one. We will have more wholistically developed men and women. We will have parenting that

involves fathering as well as mothering. But the basic reason for the preference of partnership marriage over patriarchal marriage is justice.[20]

Ruether's dream is an ecumenical, worldwide vision. It involves not simply a new economy or a new kind of marriage. It looks toward a new relationship to nature, to God, and to our fellow human beings, regardless of sex. It is a world in which no group seeks to dominate another. It is a world in which every person, male or female, can achieve full humanity.

Some Concluding Comments

It is hardly proper for a white male Protestant, even one who is sympathetic, to raise questions about a Catholic woman's feminist theology. It behooves a member of the privileged and oppressing group to listen and to repent, not to criticize. Yet there are Catholics and there are women who have raised objections to some aspects of feminist theology. We may here at least note a few of their questions and some of the ways in which Ruether might reply.

(1) Does not the word of God command women to be subordinate to men? No! Such Bible verses no more represent God's word to us today than do those which condone slavery. The enduring message of the Bible is that of justice and freedom.

(2) Are there not values women lose in the dissolution of the old patterns? To Ruether, that seems a misleading question. Of course there are joys in rearing children, she gladly agrees. Her concern is simply that these joys and tasks not be assigned exclusively to women.

(3) Does not feminist theology substitute a criterion from sociology for adherence to God's word? Isn't theology to be based on God's self-revelation, not the self-interest of one sex? Her answer is that it is traditional theology which has reflected the self-interest of one sex, the male. Ruether's objective is to present a theology which will reflect God's concern for *all* people. She is careful to avoid a reverse chauvinism.

(4) Finally, is the prophetic mission of the church to call upon the oppressed to unite and throw off their chains? Is it not rather to

summon the oppressors to repent and themselves set the down-trodden free? Ruether, however, does not deny the need for repentance by the oppressors or the importance of that call. She simply recognizes realistically that sinful human beings rarely give up privileges out of pure benevolence. It took the labor movement to produce the gains industrial workers now enjoy. It took sacrificial cooperation by Blacks themselves to bring about such improvements as we now have in civil rights. Hence a new era of justice for women will require that they work together for their cause, too.

Study Suggestions

1. Ruether's feminist theology must be understood in the light of a new, widespread concern for the rights of women. You might begin by making a list of the changes in the status of women which you yourself have observed, especially those which have occurred since 1963 when Betty Friedan wrote *The Feminine Mystique*. (pp. 71–72) What values and/or dangers do you see in them?

2. Ruether, reviewing history, says that in the nineteenth century the ideal "lady" was supposed to be "half angel, half idiot." Review what she says about sexism in history (pp. 75–78) and see if you can describe (a) what she means by this phrase and (b) what truth, if any, you find in that summary.

3. What in Ruether's review of history, especially church history, surprises you or especially catches your interest? In what ways has the church sided with the oppression of women?

4. Feminist theology will have its own standard of judgment: "The critical principle of feminist theology is the promotion of the full humanity of women. Whatever denies, diminishes, or distorts the full humanity of women is, therefore, appraised as not redemptive. . . . what does promote the full humanity of women is of the Holy." In what ways do you agree or disagree with this standard of appraising theology?

5. Like other theologians we have studied, Ruether believes her theology to be true to the real meaning of the Bible. Here are

some passages on which she does *not* build her doctrines: 1 Corinthians 11:2–9; 14:34–35; Colossians 3:18; 1 Timothy 2:11–15; 1 Peter 3:1–6. To what extent do you agree with her that these must be understood as at best incomplete understandings of God's will, still reflecting the culture of the day in which they were written?

6. At the same time Ruether does build her theology on certain principles which she sees as characteristic of what is most clearly Christian in Scripture. Be sure to review the passages and even more the basic biblical ideas cited on pp. 80–81. Review especially Matthew 20:26–27. Much of Ruether's theology is an effort to apply this teaching of Jesus to contemporary concerns, not only sexism but also racism and economic oppression. Do you think she is right to do this? If so, how well does it seem to you she succeeds?

7. As you review the doctrine-by-doctrine summary of her feminist theology, note especially what she says about the doctrines of creation and of "anthropology." What new ideas does she propose in these areas, and in what ways do these ideas seem to you to be valid or invalid?

8. How do her doctrines compare with those of the other "prophets" we have been studying?

9. In the description of Ruether's vision of the future, note especially how this wife and mother of three describes the ideal marriage as partnership. (See pp. 84–85 and compare the second question on p. 85.) To what extent is hers a desirable goal or a realistic goal?

10. In "Some Concluding Comments" the author asks four questions which have been proposed about Ruether's feminist theology. In what ways do you find the proposed answers adequate or inadequate? What do you think she might add to these answers?

11. You might ask someone active in the women's movement, perhaps a representative of the National Organization for Women (NOW), to speak to your study group. You might also ask an ordained woman to talk with you about the status of women in the church today as she sees it.

Conclusion

Biblical prophecy and subsequent Christian prophecy which seeks to carry on the biblical tradition seem frequently to involve a paradox. On the one hand, prophets are often sure that the kingdom of heaven is at hand. They already see signs of the dawning of the new day, the Day of the Lord. They call us to rejoice in foreshadowings of the glorious era already visible. Yet, on the other hand, the full coming of the kingdom always seems delayed. Injustices persist, and the next generation still needs its new prophets of hope, of warning, and of challenge.

The purpose of this brief concluding chapter is a double one. It calls upon the reader to celebrate the clear indications that God is bringing the kingdom in. The prophets we have been studying are themselves among the clearest of these hopeful signs. Yet this chapter is also to remind us of the unfinished task. Poverty, racism, and sexism are still very much with us, and there are other areas of injustice each of which still waits for another Rauschenbusch or King or Gutiérrez or Ruether.

If Walter Rauschenbusch could visit a modern factory and contrast it with the sweatshops he knew a century ago, he might almost think that the kingdom had indeed arrived. A work week of forty hours or less is taken for granted. Factories appear to be far cleaner and safer, and they are more pleasant places in which to work. The workers enjoy a standard of living Rauschenbusch never dreamed of for them. The retired receive social security and medicare benefits, and even many of the unemployed live in what might have seemed luxury to millions in the 1890s. Rauschenbusch's prayers are being answered.

Yet it is widely agreed that the power of organized labor, which won so much of this progress, is now rapidly declining. Millions are unemployed. Not only the actual number but also the percentage of our population which is below the poverty line seems to grow every year. We are so far from having achieved any semblance of economic justice in this country that we find the poorest twenty percent of our families receive only five and three-tenths percent of the national income. The lowest forty percent get only sixteen and nine-tenths percent. The top five percent, however, get fifteen and seven-tenths percent of our wealth. Numerically there are probably more Americans homeless and in bread lines today than there were a century ago.

*

In his brief ministry Martin Luther King, Jr. saw amazing progress in race relations. One wishes he could have lived on to see how much more of his dream has already come true. Here are typical examples. Just a few years ago a Black boy begged the mayor of a little Alabama town for the use of the city ballpark. It was just for one game, he pleaded, a championship contest with a neighboring community. Of course the mayor, a cousin of mine, firmly refused him. Today that Black, now a man, is himself the mayor of that town. I vividly remember seeing the run-down Black school on the back street in the little southern town in which I was reared. It seems incredible that the shiny new school in that same community, now a small city, is fully integrated. White politicians who once won elections with the slogan "segregation forever!" now openly court the votes of millions of newly registered Blacks. Formerly all-white universities now compete for good Black students, and businesses are ready to hire those who graduate.

A Jeremiah or a King, however, would not let us rest content as long as the following is true:

A black baby today is three times as likely as a white infant to die during the first year of life. . . . Because black children are more likely to be poor, they are more likely to be sick. A black child is more than two and one-half times as likely as a white child to live in dilapidated housing and is twice as likely to be on welfare. A black child's father is 70 percent more likely than a white child's father to be unemployed, and when black fathers find work they bring home an average of $70 a week less than white fathers.[1]

Any Black reader of this book will be aware, too, of evidences of prejudice not so easily described in statistical terms.

*

Paradoxically, the effectiveness of the preaching of liberation theology by Gutiérrez and others like him is shown most clearly in the intensity of the opposition it has generated. The Vatican has found it necessary to reaffirm its strong condemnation of Marxism, but even as it has done so it has condemned economic injustice in ways unheard of a century ago. The United States government pours arms into Latin America to repress revolution, but even as it does so it has sometimes brought pressure upon Latin American regimes to eliminate some of the more flagrant abuses of civil rights. So many priests and even bishops in Latin America have identified themselves with the cry for justice that it is quite possible that when the apparently inevitable revolutions occur the church may have a real chance to influence the new systems which will emerge.

The stand for economic justice, including sympathy for those seeking change, has not been confined to the Roman Catholics or to South America, as its opposition attests. By 1984 both "60 Minutes" on CBS TV and the *Reader's Digest* were warning Protestants that their National and World Councils of Churches were supporting "Marxist revolutionists" in many places. While this opposition exaggerated Protestant support for change, it was true that these councils were taking a stand for racial and economic justice around the world. Even in apartheid-ridden South Africa so many church leaders have spoken out in behalf of the oppressed that the white government there has had to arrest and imprison many. The Nobel Peace Prize in 1984 went to an Anglican Bishop for his heroic stand for justice in that troubled country. God is at work. Yet it takes a faith-inspired prophet to see many signs of hope in the third word today. What most would regard as a more realistic prophecy is this report found in *Newsweek,* August 4, 1980:

> A GRIM YEAR 2000. . . . The time: the year 2000. The place: Earth, a desolate planet slowly dying of its own accumulating follies. Half of the forests are gone; sand dunes spread where fertile farm lands once lay. Nearly 2 million species of plants, birds, insects and animals have vanished. Yet man is propagating so fast that his cities have grown as large as his nations of a century before. The bleak scenario is not science fiction, but a detailed . . . report submitted . . . last week by the State Department and the Council on Environmental Quality. . . . Hundreds of millions of people will be hungry. In some parts of the Mideast, Africa and Asia, the report predicts, "the quantity of food available to the poorest groups of people will simply be insufficient to permit children to reach normal body weight and intelligence."[2]

Already, we are told that every year fifteen million children die of malnutrition and related diseases, but the combination of exploding population and dwindling farm land seems to promise as the future for millions only disease and even mass starvation. "Global 2000," the report so briefly summarized, points to closely related concerns. Our chapter on Gutiérrez reminded us of widespread poverty in the third world. Basic to that problem are the twin threats posed by the rapid expansion of the population and the savage destruction of our natural resources. Oil and gas cannot last long into the next century. The Sahara desert is growing over more and more of Africa, and forests and water supplies are disappearing. While the prospects are in some ways encouraging for the currently affluent nations of Europe and North America, the future of the peoples of Latin America, Africa, and Asia seems grim indeed.

---

*

In the twenty years following the writing of Betty Friedan's *The Feminine Mystique* the progress toward women's liberation has been phenomenal. A commencement speaker at a women's college could note that fifty-three percent of all women hold jobs, the number of never-married women who work having increased fifty-eight percent in just ten years. While at one time many women still held only clerical jobs, by 1983 one-fourth of all working women had professional, technical, or administrative and managerial employment. By that year more women than men were entering college, and such once all-male institutions as the schools of law and medicine had one-fourth or even one-half female students. More and more women have won political office, the Supreme Court includes a woman judge, and Geraldine Ferraro has been the Democrats' candidate for vice president. God is setting women free.

Nevertheless it is still true that women average making only fifty-nine cents for every dollar paid to men. The Equal Rights Amendment failed to win the support of the required two-thirds of the states. Also, the fact that more and more women have entered the work force has not meant that they have achieved complete liberation. A writer in the January 1984 *Ladies Home Journal* reports on a survey, "Clearly the housewife's blues have given way to the working mother's frustration—and even rage." Only half the husbands surveyed always or frequently share in the housework, even though the wife may work outside the home as many hours as he does. Many women have simply added work outside the home to the tasks of cook, housekeeper, and mother.

We have focused on four issues, but there are others of equal concern. We have noted only in passing the desperate problem of ecology. The rapidly multiplying proportion of old people represents another kind of challenge. Blacks are not the only ones in this country who are victims of racial prejudice. Of course, there remains the threat which may eliminate all the others and all of us with it, nuclear war. (One estimate is that the United States and the Soviet Union now have between them some fifty thousand nuclear weapons. It would take only about three hundred and fifty of these to destroy both countries completely!)

This book, therefore, is written both in celebration of four "major prophets" of our time and in the faith that God will raise up others. Yet it is also part of God's plan that there should be "minor prophets" who in their lesser ways will also voice God's message of hope and judgment. There were many prophets in the early church whose names we will never know. Perhaps each reader of this book is called by God to be a prophetic witness to the coming kingdom of justice and love. Moses had a vision about this: "Would that all the LORD's people were prophets" (Num. 11:29). "Your sons and your daughters shall prophesy," Joel promised (3:28), and at Pentecost Peter could see that prophecy coming true (Acts 2:17).

God will raise up many more prophets to bear in diverse ways their witness to the coming kingdom. This book is written in the hope and faith that some of us will be among them and millions more of us will respond actively to their message.

Study Suggestions

The conclusion of this book is intended to help you do three things: it can help you do a brief review of the concerns of the four prophets who have been its subject; it reminds us that their work has not been in vain, that God is doing many of the things for which they have prayed; and it is also intended to challenge us to the continuing work for the causes they championed and other causes like them. Consider what these thinkers have said and done, praise God for the progress that has been made, and consider how you may also serve as a witness to the coming kingdom of God. Here are some things that might be done as you come to the end of this volume.

1. Review the book. Which ideas have been most interesting to you and to different members of the study group, if you have one? Which of these prophets' books would you like to study now?

Which of their causes would you most like to learn more about as it touches your own community and church?

2. In relation to each of the four chapters, what signs of progress can you and others point to? Can you tell stories of God being at work in ways you have seen: bringing justice to the poor, breaking down racial barriers, or bringing greater freedom to women? Try to think of specific examples of the evidence that God is bringing the changes of which our prophets have seen visions. Are there also signs of judgment upon us for our failure to heed some part of our prophets' messages?

3. Most importantly, consider what things still need to be done. What do you think one of our prophets might propose if she or he were to visit your church? What might be a next step you individually or your group might take toward acting on the messages of these four? What other causes ought we to study and to work for?

Notes

Chapter 1

1. Walter Rauschenbusch, *Christianizing the Social Order* (New York: Macmillan, 1912), p. 51.
2. As quoted by Dores Robinson Sharpe, *Walter Rauschenbusch* (New York: Macmillan, 1942), p. 43.
3. Ibid.
4. Walter Rauschenbusch, *Christianity and the Social Crisis* (New York: Macmillan, 1907), p. xv.
5. Quoted by Harry Emerson Fosdick in the introduction to *A Rauschenbusch Reader*, edited by Benson Y. Landis (New York: Harper, 1957), pp. xv–xvi.
6. Henry George, *Progress and Poverty: An Inquiry into the Cause of Industrial Depressions and of Increase of Want with Increase of Wealth—The Remedy* (New York: Robert Schalkenbach Foundation, 1942 [originally published 1879]), p. 552.
7. Walter Rauschenbusch, "The Kingdom of God," *Cleveland's Young Men* (January 9, 1913), as quoted by Vernon Parker Bodein, *The Social Gospel of Walter Rauschenbusch and Its Relation to Religious Education* (New Haven: Yale University, 1944), pp. 7–8.
8. Rauschenbusch, *Christianizing the Social Order*, p. 93.
9. Ibid., p. 49.
10. Rauschenbusch, *Christianity and the Social Crisis*, p. 8.

11. Walter Rauschenbusch, *A Theology for the Social Gospel* (New York: Macmillan, 1917), p. 50.
12. Ibid., pp. 96–97.
13. Ibid., p. 143.
14. Ibid., p. 149.
15. Ibid., pp. 154–55.
16. Ibid., p. 142.
17. Rauschenbusch, *Christianizing the Social Order*, pp. 412–13.
18. Ibid., p. 235.
19. Walter Rauschenbusch, from *For the Right*, II/2 (November 1890), as quoted by Vernon Parker Bodein, *The Social Gospel of Walter Rauschenbusch and Its Relation to Religious Education*, pp. 10–11.
20. Rauschenbusch, *Christianity and the Social Crisis*, p. 422.
21. Rauschenbusch, *Christianizing the Social Order*, p. 29.

Chapter 2

1. Martin Luther King, Jr., *Stride Toward Freedom: The Montgomery Story* (New York: Harper, 1958), p. 19.
2. Ibid., p. 20. [I have written in this essay of the influence of Rauschenbusch and Gandhi on King. For a full discussion of other scholarly influences on King's thought see John J. Ansbro, *Martin Luther King, Jr.: The Making of a Mind* (Maryknoll, NY: Orbis, 1982).]
3. Ibid., p. 91.
4. Ibid., p. 17.
5. Ibid., p. 60.
6. Ibid., p. 62.
7. Mahatma Gandhi, as quoted in C. F. Andrews, *Mahatma Gandhi's Ideas: Including Selections from His Writings* (New York: Macmillan, 1930), p. 192.
8. King, *Stride Toward Freedom*, p. 97.
9. Ibid., p. 84.
10. Ibid., pp. 134–35.
11. Martin Luther King, Jr., *Why We Can't Wait* (New York: Harper, 1963), p. 103.
12. Chap. 5, pp. 77–100, contains the entire letter from which the quotations in this chapter have been excerpted.
13. The best account of the Selma campaign is that of David J. Garrow, *Protest at Selma: Martin Luther King, Jr., and the Voting Rights Act of 1965* (New Haven: Yale University, 1978).
14. As quoted by Stephen B. Oates, *Let the Trumpet Sound: The Life of Martin Luther King, Jr.* (New York: Harper, 1982), p. 486.

15. King, *Stride Toward Freedom*, p. 36.
16. Martin Luther King, Jr., *Where Do We Go from Here: Chaos or Community?* (New York: Harper, 1967), p. 190.
17. Ibid., p. 205.
18. As quoted by Stephen B. Oates, *Let the Trumpet Sound*, p. 364.
19. King, *Where Do We Go from Here?*, p. 191.
20. As quoted by Stephen B. Oates, *Let the Trumpet Sound*, p. 261.

Chapter 3

1. As quoted by Phillip Berryman, "Camilo Torres: Revolutionary-Theologian," *Commonweal* 96 (April 21, 1972) 164, 165.
2. As quoted by Gustavo Gutiérrez, *A Theology of Liberation: History, Politics and Salvation*, translated and edited by Sister Caridad Inda and John Eagleson (Maryknoll, NY: Orbis, 1973), p. 305 n. 48.
3. As quoted by Gustavo Gutiérrez, *The Power of the Poor in History*, translated by Robert R. Barr (Maryknoll, NY: Orbis, 1983), p. 63.
4. Christine Gudorf, "The Quiet Strength of Liberation Theology," *Commonweal* 108 (June 15, 1984) 366.
5. Much of the biographical information here comes from Robert McAfee Brown, *Gustavo Gutiérrez* (Atlanta: John Knox, 1980).
6. "Jesus the Liberator?" *Time* (September 1, 1975) 34.
7. Gutiérrez, *A Theology of Liberation*, p. 308.
8. "Jesus the Liberator?" *Time* (September 1, 1975) 34.
9. Dow Kirkpatrick, "Liberation Theologians and Third World Demands: A Dialogue with Gustavo Gutiérrez and Javier Inguiñiz," *The Christian Century* 93 (May 12, 1976) p. 460.
10. Gutiérrez, *The Power of the Poor in History*, p. 69.
11. Gutiérrez, *A Theology of Liberation*, p. 35.
12. Ibid., pp. 36–37.
13. Ibid., p. 36.
14. Ibid., p. 178.
15. Gutiérrez, *The Power of the Poor in History*, p. 66.
16. Gutiérrez, *A Theology of Liberation*, p. 205.
17. Gutiérrez, *The Power of the Poor in History*, p. 47.
18. Gustavo Gutiérrez, *We Drink from Our Own Wells: The Spiritual Journey of a People*, translated by Matthew J. O'Connell (Maryknoll, NY: Orbis, 1984), p. 38.
19. Gutiérrez, *The Power of the Poor in History*, pp. 52-53.
20. Gutiérrez, *We Drink from Our Own Wells*, p. 137.
21. Gutiérrez, *The Power of the Poor in History*, p. 21.
22. Ibid., p. 81.
23. As quoted by Robert McAfee Brown, "Drinking from Our Own Wells," *The Christian Century* 101 (May 9, 1984) 483.

24. James H. Cone, *A Black Theology of Liberation* (Philadelphia: Lippincott, 1970).
25. After reading this paragraph Robert McAfee Brown, a leading exponent of liberation theology, wrote me that "at least for Gustavo and those in Latin America, the notion of finding an alternative 'between' capitalism and socialism is not attractive. They call it *tercerismo* (a third way), and their complaint is that proponents of *tercerismo* always capitulate when the going gets tough. It is also the way opponents of liberation theology try to co-opt the term, claiming to be for 'true' liberation, which is spiritual liberation and which can therefore live under any kind of economic arrangement."

Chapter 4

1. Betty Friedan, *The Feminine Mystique* (New York: Dell, 1963), p. 11.
2. Ibid.
3. Ibid., p. 364.
4. Mary Daly, *Beyond God the Father: Toward a Philosophy of Women's Liberation* (Boston: Beacon, 1973), p. 73.
5. Ibid., p. 96.
6. Rosemary Radford Ruether, "What Is Shaping My Theology: Social Sin," *Commonweal* 108 (January 30, 1981) 46–47.
7. Ibid., p. 47.
8. As quoted by Rosemary Radford Ruether, *Sexism and God-Talk: Toward a Feminist Theology* (Boston: Beacon, 1983), p. 167.
9. Rosemary Radford Ruether, *Mary, the Feminine Face of the Church* (Philadelphia: Westminster, 1977), p. 64.
10. Ibid., p. 86.
11. Ruether, *Sexism and God-Talk*, p. 13.
12. Ibid., pp. 18–19.
13. Ibid., p. 24.
14. Ibid., p. 120.
15. Ruether, "What Is Shaping My Theology: Social Sin," p. 47.
16. Ruether, *Sexism and God-Talk*, p. 161.
17. Ibid., pp. 111–12.
18. Rosemary Radford Ruether and Eleanor McLaughlin (eds.), *Women of Spirit: Female Leadership in the Jewish and Christian Traditions* (New York: Simon and Schuster, 1979), p. 380.
19. Rosemary Radford Ruether, "Sexism and the Theology of Liberation: Nature, Fall and Salvation as Seen from the Experience of Women," *The Christian Century* 90 (December 12, 1973) 1227.
20. Wolfgang Roth and Rosemary Radford Ruether, *The Liberating Bond: Covenants Biblical and Contemporary, Use Guide* by Elizabeth L. McWhorter (New York: Friendship, 1978), p. 57.

Conclusion

1. Marian Wright Edelman, "The Budget and the People," *Christianity & Crisis* (April 13, 1981) 104.
2. Fay Willey with William J. Cook, "A Grim Year 2000," *Newsweek* (August 4, 1980) 38.

Bibliography

If you would like to do further study of the four modern prophets described in this book, here are some suggestions for further reading. This list makes no claim to being a full bibliography. Rosemary Radford Ruether is the author or subject of more than four hundred books, articles, and reviews, and the literature on Martin Luther King is, of course, enormous. The listing here includes most of the works which I have cited in this book, with some of the more significant items annotated briefly.

Chapter 1

Rauschenbusch, Walter. *Christianity and the Social Crisis.* New York: Macmillan, 1907.
This is Rauschenbusch's first book, a pioneering call for justice.
————. *Christianizing the Social Order.* New York: Macmillan, 1912.
————. *A Theology for the Social Gospel.* New York: Macmillan, 1917 [reprinted Nashville: Abingdon, 1945]. This is a clear, systematic, and forceful summary of Rauschenbusch's social gospel, a classic work.
Bodein, Vernon Parker. *The Social Gospel of Walter Rauschenbusch and Its Relation to Religious Education.* New Haven: Yale University, 1944.
George, Henry. *Progress and Poverty: An Inquiry into the Cause of Industrial Depressions and of Increase of Want with Increase of Wealth—The Remedy.* New York: Robert Schalkbenbach Foundation, 1942 [originally published 1879].

Landis, Benson Y. (ed.). *A Rauschenbusch Reader.* New York: Harper, 1957.

Sharpe, Dores Robinson. *Walter Rauschenbusch.* New York: Macmillan, 1942. A devoted student has written a very readable biography of the great teacher.

Chapter 2

King, Martin Luther, Jr. *Stride Toward Freedom: The Montgomery Story.* New York: Harper, 1958. King's own autobiography describes his early life and his first great campaign, the bus boycott in Montgomery, Alabama. It tells, too, how he developed his concept of nonviolent resistance. It is fascinating reading, the best place to begin

————. *Why We Can't Wait.* New York: Harper, 1963. Also autobiographical, this includes King's account of the Birmingham campaign and the complete text of his famous "Letter from a Birmingham Jail."

————. *Where Do We Go from Here: Chaos or Community?* New York: Harper, 1967. King's third and last book points to the need for continued work for economic justice rather than war.

Andrews, C. F. *Mahatma Gandhi's Ideas: Including Selections from His Writings.* New York: Macmillan, 1930.

Ansbro, John J. *Martin Luther King, Jr.: The Making of a Mind.* Maryknoll, NY: Orbis, 1982.

Garrow, David J. *Protest at Selma: Martin Luther King, Jr., and the Voting Rights Act of 1965.* New Haven: Yale University, 1978.

Oates, Stephen B. *Let the Trumpet Sound: The Life of Martin Luther King, Jr.* New York: Harper, 1982. Oates has written a readable and moving biography of King.

Chapter 3

Gutiérrez, Gustavo. *A Theology of Liberation: History, Politics and Salvation,* translated and edited by Sister Caridad Inda and John Eagleson. Maryknoll, NY: Orbis, 1973. This is the pioneering, classic work of Gutiérrez which presents his thought systematically, the book that did most to make his ideas known in North America.

————. *The Power of the Poor in History,* translated by Robert R. Barr. Maryknoll, NY: Orbis, 1983.

————. *We Drink from Our Own Wells: The Spiritual Journey of a People,* translated by Matthew J. O'Connell. Maryknoll, NY: Orbis, 1984. Here Gutiérrez describes the devotional life which grows out of involvement with the poor in their struggle for justice.

Berryman, Phillip. "Camilo Torres: Revolutionary-Theologian," *Commonweal* 96 (April 21, 1972) 164–66.

Brown, Robert McAfee. *Gustavo Gutiérrez*. Atlanta: John Knox, 1980. This brief and interestingly written introduction to the life and thought of Gutiérrez is by one of his friends. Brown is a leading proponent of liberation theology in the United States.

————. "Drinking from Our Own Wells," *The Christian Century* 101 (May 9, 1984) 483–86.

Cone, James H. *A Black Theology of Liberation*. Philadelphia: Lippincott, 1970.

Gudorf, Christine. "The Quiet Strength of Liberation Theology," *Commonweal* 108 (June 15, 1984) 365–67.

Kirkpatrick, Dow. "Liberation Theologians and Third World Demands: A Dialogue with Gustavo Gutiérrez and Javier Iguiñiz," *The Christian Century* 93 (May 12, 1976) 456–60.

"Jesus the Liberator?" *Time* (September 1, 1975) 34.

Chapter 4

Ruether, Rosemary Radford. "Sexism and the Theology of Liberation: Nature, Fall and Salvation as Seen from the Experience of Women," *The Christian Century* 90 (December 12, 1973) 1224–29.

————. *New Woman, New Earth: Sexist Ideologies and Human Liberation*. New York: Seabury, 1975. Ruether exposes many of the sources of sexism in society and the church. The book forcefully links the cause of feminism to concern for economic and racial justice, ecology, and peace.

————. *Mary, the Feminine Face of the Church*. Philadelphia: Westminster, 1977.

Roth, Wolfgang, and Rosemary Radford Ruether, with Elizabeth L. McWhorter. *The Liberating Bond: Covenants Biblical and Contemporary*. New York: Friendship, 1978.

Ruether, Rosemary Radford, and Eleanor McLaughlin (eds.). *Women of Spirit: Female Leadership in the Jewish and Christian Traditions*. New York: Simon and Schuster, 1979.

Ruether, Rosemary Radford. "What Is Shaping My Theology: Social Sin," *Commonweal* 108 (January 30, 1981) 46–48. This article includes some autobiographical material as it relates to her concerns for justice.

————. *Sexism and God-Talk: Toward a Feminist Theology*. Boston: Beacon, 1983. A comprehensive, systematic summary of Christian theology from the perspective of the author, this is the fullest presentation of her mature thought.

Ruether writes so frequently for both *Commonweal* and *The Christian*

Century that the reader might profitably consult current issues of these two periodicals for her most recent contributions.

Daly, Mary. *Beyond God the Father: Toward a Philosophy of Women's Liberation.* Boston: Beacon, 1973.
Friedan, Betty. *The Feminine Mystique.* New York: Dell, 1963.

Conclusion

Edelman, Marian Wright. "The Budget and the People," *Christianity and Crisis* (April 13, 1981) 103–6.
Willey, Fay with William J. Cook. "A Grim Year 2000," *Newsweek* (August 4, 1980) 38.